Woman Pastor

Woman Pastor

The Seasons and Sacrifice of One Woman's Ministry

Betty Anne Johnson

© 2019, Betty Anne Johnson

All rights reserved.

No part of this publication may be reproduced, stored in a retrieval system, or transmitted in any form or by any means - electronic, mechanical, photocopy, recording or any other - except for brief quotations in printed reviews, without the prior written permission of the publisher.

All Scripture quotations, are taken from the HOLY BIBLE, NEW INTERNATIONAL VERSION ®. NIV ®. Copyright 1973, 1978, 1984 by the International Bible Society. Used by permission of Zondervan Publishing House. All rights reserved.

ISBN

To every woman pastor.
The ones who tried and failed.
The ones who struggled alone.
The ones who fought and won.
The ones who gave up the fight.
And the ones for whom every day
as a pastor was absolute joy.
You are heroes in the Kingdom.

For the realization of this book, I am indebted to:
    David L. Smith, advisor, editor
    Connie L. Stewart, reader
    Laura Zigrang, reader
and each of the congregations for whom I was Pastor. Each one helped me grow an learn what I would otherwise have never known. I was truly blessed by each one.

Contents

Preface..ix
1 In the Beginning...1
2 Growing Up Fast..10
3 The Call 22
4 Don't Cry..36
5 The Fall..44
6 Guilt and Grace 56
7 Arrested!...67
8 Ice Cream 79
9 Moving On 85
10 Interlude..98
11 Gentle Love...110
12 Tough Love 121
13 Joyous Love 149
14 Home 158
15 Looking Back 167
16 Autonomy...170
About the Author 173

PREFACE

I am a woman. I have been a pastor for over 20 years. Undoubtedly, there are women pastors out there who have more experience than I. There are women pastors who can articulate stories similar to the ones I'm about to tell, much better than I. This is *my* story. If you are a woman pastor, you will no doubt see yourself in some of my story. If you are a church member whose pastor is a woman, you may find yourself in the pew or on the sidewalk of my story. If you are a denominational leader, you may resonate with the most difficult parts of my story. If you believe women should not be pastors, you may change your mind, or you may not, once you read my story.

I hope that in sharing *my* story, *your* story may become a little clearer or a little less frightening. Pastoral ministry is not for the faint of heart. Pastoral ministry for a woman has unique role sets and cautions that can make the strongest heart cringe. Being a woman in ministry is also filled with indescribable beauty, unparalleled joy, and inescapable freedom.

What you are about to read will, at times, seem like fiction. I assure you, it is not. Nor is it an avenue to condone or condemn anybody's actions but my own. God will be the judge of all that has happened with me, by me, and to me. I pray that your ministry journey will be as sweet as mine has been when God whispers to your soul, "Hang on, dear child. There's a bumpy road ahead."

Soli Deo Gloria,
(Rev. Dr.) Betty Anne Johnson,
Truro, NS CANADA
November 2019

x

1
IN THE BEGINNING

I was born in a small town in Nova Scotia, Canada and lived there until I was the ripe old age of nine years. Life was good in our small town. At least we thought it was. If there was financial hardship, we kids didn't know about it. Our family went to a very conservative church. The weekends centered around church and church activities. Very often there would be a couple from church along with their children seated at our table for Sunday dinner. Just as often, our family would be at another home for dinner. There was always a Sunday evening church service and after that service, it was not uncommon for sandwiches and tea to be served at someone's home. Birthday party guests were church kids and the two girls who lived across the street. Summer vacation was at the church campgrounds.

In the Beginning

When missionaries came to visit, they enjoyed my parents' hospitality for an evening meal or lodging for a week, whichever was needed. Those were the days of revival meetings in churches and when the annual revival meeting came to our town, our home was always open for hosting the visiting evangelists or musicians. It wasn't unusual for me, after I had been sent to bed, to sneak out of my room and sit at the top of the stairs as quietly as I could, in order to listen to the conversation and the music (there was always music) coming up from the living room.

You might say we were the typical church-going family in the early 1960's. Mom's gift of hospitality was unrivaled. Dad was quiet, almost shy, but when he spoke there was tremendous wisdom in his words that made people listen. My older sister took more after my dad. She was a compliant child, well-spoken, obedient, and she kept her side of our bedroom clean and tidy. I was the typical middle child. I didn't really care if my side of our room was tidy - there were adventures to take and things to do beyond mundane tasks like hanging up clothes or making a bed.

I was drawn to nature and its beauty. I loved to play outside by myself. Mom said I would play quite happily for hours in the back yard. My brother was the youngest and the only boy. I don't remember much about him in those younger years. Maybe that's because I got in a lot of trouble trying to boss him around. Mostly though, I think it was because my sister and I were often doing things together, so maybe my brother just got left out a lot. I do remember building a "fort" with him and some of the other neighborhood kids up at the top of the hill where our street came to an end. And I remember riding our bikes up and down our street. It was as close to an idyllic childhood as any adult could hope to recall.

Unfortunately, hard times in the Maritimes became a reality for our family when my father lost his job as an auto-body repair man at Nelson Motors. Dad said they were hiring younger guys who had college degrees. I remember him sitting on the sofa with his head in his hands. It was exactly like a few years before when he came home from work for lunch and Mom had to tell him his dad had died of a heart attack. I was standing at the living room door, seeing Dad sitting on the couch with his head in his hands. I knew something was terribly wrong and I just stood there and watched him. I couldn't imagine what had happened of course, but even as young as I was, I knew it was time to be very quiet because that was what Dad needed right then.

Dad sat again, head in his hands. I guess we never really appreciate as children, what our parents go through as adults worrying about paying the bills and providing for their children. I was eight when it happened. Mom and Dad sold the home they had lovingly built themselves. It was a two-story family home with a center entry and one long center staircase that lead to three large bedrooms and a huge bathroom on the second floor. Mom and Dad did most of the work on the house themselves.

In the Beginning

From the front door, our home opened to a living room and back bedroom to the left and a formal dining room and eat-in kitchen to the right.

When Dad was painting he took the time to explain to me how to cut into the edges and to keep from applying too thick a coat. I was very young, but I still remember Dad taking the time to show me how to paint. He warned my sister and I one day that he had just painted the toilet seat so we should not use the bathroom without telling him first so he could make sure the paint was dry. But children sometimes get desperate and forget instructions and that's exactly what I had done within the hour. I was so afraid to yell for Dad but there I was "stuck" to the toilet seat and I could feel myself slowly slipping because the enamel paint was definitely not yet dry! I finally cried for help, was dutifully cleaned up with paint thinner of some sort, and the bathroom door was locked from the inside!

After Mom and Dad had to sell our home, they found rentable spaces here and there for a family of five, and then finally did what a lot of families did back then when everything else failed. They sold most of their furniture and packed up our few remaining belongings and moved west, to the "land of milk and honey" - Ontario. Well, if it wasn't the land of milk and honey, it was at least the land of lower unemployment and better pay. And there was an offer of free rent from a kind and generous great aunt which made the move hard to resist for two very lost and struggling young parents with three growing children.

It was a Monday morning in September, when Mom, Dad, and three little kids loaded themselves into their family car with a small, homemade trailer hitched behind and headed west. On their knees in the backseat (yes it was before seatbelts were mandatory), three distraught children were peering out the back window, tears streaming down their cheeks, singing, "farewell to Nova Scotia, my sea-bound coast, let your mountains dark and dreary be . . ." Mom and Dad had no idea what lay ahead but one thing was certain, they couldn't survive on what they were leaving behind.

Cottage living in Ontario was vastly different than small town Nova Scotia. Aunt Mabel's cottage had two kitchens, two living rooms, two bathrooms, four bedrooms, and a private beach. We lived in one of the most desirable locations of Ontario's cottage country for a year. It didn't take Mom and Dad long to find jobs in what to us was the big city. It was a suburb of Toronto. We quickly became latch-key kids. Mom and Dad left very early for work, often waking us up for school just before they left. They came home from work exhausted but grateful they had jobs. Dad was working in an auto-body shop as he had done all his life.

In the Beginning

Mom was working at a grocery store as a cashier. Summer at the cottage was especially nice for us kids. We enjoyed the beach and outside activities, especially badminton on the front lawn. We were still too young to know the reality of our situation and Mom and Dad were careful to shelter us from the heavy burdens they carried.

After a year, we moved into the big city. Aunt Mabel had divided her Rosedale mansion into apartments. When one of her tenants moved out of their one-bedroom apartment, she offered it to us. It was cramped quarters, but it was closer for Mom and Dad for work so we left the upscale cottage country and headed for the downtown affluent district. I loved living right beside Aunt Mabel. She was kind and generous, and I still remember her beautiful smile. She took a cruise around the world every two years. I remember being given permission to have a short visit with her the same night she got back from one of her cruises because I had missed her so much. After school every day I rushed home to be with Aunt Mabel where I was allowed to watch television, a worldly indulgence our family had not yet experienced.

Mom and Dad did well at their jobs. Dad became foreman of the auto-body shop. Mom became head cashier at the grocery store. They found a house to rent just outside the city suburbs so we escaped the pace of the city and settled into a quieter lifestyle. Much to the joy of us kids, the house Mom and Dad rented came with the agreement that we would look after the owner's little dog. It was a one-year lease. It was a tight-knit community which felt more like home than we'd experienced for a while. Mom and Dad were not as far from work so our routine included more family time and even community events. They also found a church in the city that was the same denomination as we left in Nova Scotia. We began attending regularly.

Life once again centered around church and church activities. Even though I was a little too young yet for youth group, I was often allowed to go, likely because my older sister promised to watch out for me. When anything was going on at the church, I wanted to be there. We were faithfully taken to youth group in the back of a pickup truck every Friday night. I was given a ride to prayer meeting and choir practice by an older single woman in the church. At least, she seemed older to me. Sometimes on Saturday night, there would be carloads of kids heading to the Stouffville Youth Center for music and fellowship. These were fun, high-energy days. I was 12 going on 21.

After our year of country living, we moved to an apartment on a busy street in the suburbs of Toronto. Mom and Dad were doing well at their jobs which meant a greater sense of security for them. We went from the apartment to a house, and I went from elementary school to high school, all in the same general area. We stayed at the same schools, went to the same church, and maintained the same friends for over five years. When I graduated high school, there was only one direction on my mind. I headed back to the east coast for college.

I loved college. It was like being at camp meeting all year long because I was with my east coast friends from church and camp. I enrolled in the B.A. in Ministry program. I felt safe and accepted and got involved in whatever I could, especially music. In high school, I had been in choir, band, orchestra, and on the music council. I received the Grade 13 Ring Award for music when I finished grade 12. In college, I joined the choir, and even had the joy of going on a choir tour during my first year there. I loved music and would have liked to have been more involved but the caliber of musical talent at college far surpassed my high school accomplishments. Even though I felt like I tried hard, I never measured up. I was, however, content just to be in the choir. When the choir director, who was also our music teacher, left for another school at the end of my first year at college, he called each of his choir members into the choir room where he had a parting chat with us. He told me there was one thing he could say about me. I was gullible. I didn't really know what he meant, but I realize now, he had spoken a word of truth.

Back at home, my sister got married and moved to Nova Scotia with her husband and two small children. My little brother quit school, got married young, and soon followed my sister back to Nova Scotia. I came home from two years of college and went to work intending to return to school when I could support myself. I saw an ad in the newspaper and thought it was to be a secretary at a radio station. It was actually a large electronics company that manufactured radios for airplanes and military equipment. I applied and landed my first full-time job.

 As soon as I settled into work, I headed to a local bank to get a loan for the huge amount of $1500. That is what Mom and Dad said it cost to have me at college for those two years. I wanted to pay them back. I'll never forget stealthily presenting the check to my father as he sat at the dining table in our little house. I can still see the suppressed but sweet grin on Daddy's face. It was one of the proudest moments of my life. Little did I realize on that day, that returning to college was a pipe dream, and that within the year ahead, I would be married to my boss from work who was 23 years my senior. I was no longer 12 going on 21. I was 20 going on 44.

2
GROWING UP FAST

My new husband was a kind and gentle soul who at first, seemed shy and vulnerable. I was working for him when his second wife died of cancer. He had divorced his first wife after adopting two children in the hope that the addition of children to nurture would help mend their failing marriage. That seldom works however, and the marriage ended while the children were still very young. Wife number two was several years younger. They were together for five years, and married for one when she succumbed to cancer. I was wife number three. My brother told me he thought I was "awful brave" to marry a guy whose first two wives had died. He hadn't realized that Mike was divorced and widowed.

Betty Anne Johnson

I had worked for him for about a month and a half when I received a phone call from Mike telling me he wouldn't be in to work because his wife had died over the weekend. I felt terrible for him and yet the secretary sitting next to me at work said it was likely for the best. I was horrified that she would say such a cruel thing but then I heard it from a couple of others at work and someone told me she had cancer and had suffered a long time. I ordered flowers in her memory and asked my father to drive me to the funeral home to pay my respects. I slipped into the funeral home and offered Mike my sympathy. He showed me that my flowers had arrived and thanked me for them. And I left.

By the time Mike returned to work, plans were underway for the company Christmas party. While I was filing in his office, he asked me if I would go with him. I said I'd love to. Later that afternoon, he walked quickly by my work station and a piece of paper floated from his hand onto my desk. I opened the piece of paper to find hand-printed words, "How about Friday night?"

Friday night, over dinner, Mike asked me how old I was. I had just turned 20 two weeks before. He responded that at least I wasn't a teenager. After dinner, we went to a night club in downtown Toronto. If I remember right, it was called Stop33. There I had my first taste of alcohol, sherry, ordered for me by my date. When we went to leave, I tripped slightly on one of the two small stairs leading out of the club to the elevators. I'm not sure if I tripped because the alcohol got to me right away or because it was dark in the club so I missed a stair. What I do know is that first date led to 15 years in my life that I least expected.

Mike said he was a Christian and he was willing to attend church with me. After we were married he told me he considered himself a Christian with a little "c." I realize now that he was trying to tell me he wasn't another specific religion so that made him "Christian." In fact, the standing joke with Mike was that he had to go through three ministers in order to get me. We started dating in November. By Christmas he had bought me a ring with my birthstone in it. I was terrified when I realized I had a ring box from Mike. I was relieved and very pleased when I saw that it was a lovely birthstone ring. By February however, the diamond arrived. It was nice to wear an engagement ring. Those were the days when you were considered to be in danger of becoming an "old maid" if you weren't wearing a diamond by the time you were 20 or 21. I hadn't had much luck with boys, or boyfriends, and my own best friend was already engaged so I was in danger of being left behind. I wanted to have a long engagement and a Fall wedding, but Mike convinced me that we should get married in early June so that we would be free to vacation together during the summer.

Before our wedding day arrived, we visited my sister and brother and their families in the east coast. We stayed with my sister and on Sunday morning we went to church. I have no idea what the message was about but after the service was over and we had been dismissed, I decided to go to the altar to pray. I took my engagement ring off and laid it on the altar. It was the second time I had questioned my engagement. But this time I was not just questioning, I was ready to end it. An arm came around my shoulder as I prayed and surrendered my relationship to God. When I told the pastor what I intended to do, he counseled me not to be hasty. He said I would have to make it clear to Mike that God came first in my life. I can't remember if he prayed with me then or not. I imagine he did. I came back to my sister's place to a very nervous Mike. He was relieved to discover that everything was okay. Later that afternoon we headed for the airport and home. On the flight home I told him about my conversation at the altar that morning with the pastor. He seemed fine with the fact that I was intent on making sure God came first in my life. I didn't realize just how difficult that would be.

As part of our wedding plans, I had asked a former pastor to perform the ceremony. When I called to ask him, he said that he would be happy to do so. When I asked about pre-marital counseling, he said he wouldn't counsel us before marriage but he reserved the right to counsel us after. He lived a distance away which would have made pre-marital sessions difficult. I sometimes wonder if my desire for pre-marital counseling included the hope of an end to the engagement. I didn't want to hurt Mike but I instinctively knew that the road I was on was a dangerous one. With the pastor at the altar with me in the east coast, the pastor who agreed to marry us, and the pastor of the church I attended, Mike certainly had the right to feel like he had been well vetted before receiving my hand in marriage.

I vividly remember on my wedding day seeing my reflection in the car window as I sat in the passenger seat of the car Dad was driving to take us to the church. As we stopped for a red light, every ounce of my being wanted to become the runaway bride, but it was too late. I saw a pedestrian cross to our side of the street, look in the car at me and smile. This time it was me. I was the bride. And there was nothing I could do about it. That night, with us both exhausted, I slung myself across the hotel room bed and literally prayed, "My God! What have I done?"

The Bahamas were beautiful. We met other newlyweds, enjoyed the beauty of the islands, and Mike went SCUBA diving while I snorkeled overhead. When we returned a week later, I called Mom. She told me there was mail for me from my denominational mission headquarters. While I was in college, I felt a full-time call to be a missionary and sent in my application. I watched the mail for months and finally, having heard nothing, thought I must not have been acceptable, or my application hadn't gotten to the right place.

I asked Mom to open the letter and read it to me. It was an invitation from the mission board inviting me to begin the process of becoming a missionary to Sierra Leone. My heart broke into a million pieces. I got off the phone and told Mike. He said he would hate to lose his wife just a week after he had married her. I prayed through most of that night. The next day, I called the pastor who officiated our wedding and asked if he had sent the license in already. He had. All those times, right up to a week before our wedding day, when I wanted to call it off, came flooding back. Someone I shared my burden with said the call was bound to come sooner or later and God could have made sure it came before I got married, but he didn't. That advice resonated somewhere deep in my spirit so I determined I needed to stay in the situation in which I found myself and be the best wife I could be. Perhaps I had misinterpreted what I thought was God's call for me to be a missionary.

Our first year being married was filled with making new friendships, traveling, and me training to be a SCUBA diver. We went to church most Sundays. I was generally quite content and happy. We visited Mom and Dad often or went to visit Mike's mom in cottage country. Mike's two children seemed to accept me. We saw them almost every other weekend and either took them to visit their Nana or took them out for a meal. Married life wasn't so bad and maybe I would be okay after all.

Mike told me early on in our relationship that I would "grow up fast." I guess that's what he was hoping would happen but while I could act grown up on the outside, I still had the mind of a gullible, naive, sheltered 21 year old. For our first anniversary, Mike said he wanted to surprise me. We went back to the restaurant we had gone on our first date. I thought that was sweet. After dinner, before we went to Stop33 however, he told me he had another place he wanted to take me first. It was a strip club. To this day, I don't know why he wanted to take me there, other than to fulfill his male fantasies. Maybe that's what he had in mind when he told me I would grow up fast. Maybe that was his idea of growing up. We had been to a movie just a few weeks earlier that he thought "would be good" and I insisted on leaving after the first ten minutes. The movie was filled with sexual violence and degradation right from the start. On our first anniversary night, when we came out of the strip club, I told Mike I would rather not go to Stop33 and would prefer to just go home. I would soon learn the movie and the strip club were just the beginning of my "growing up fast."

Betty Anne Johnson

One of Mike's goals, even before we were married, was to get a transfer with his company to England. He continued to campaign for the transfer and it was granted to him during the second year of our marriage. In the Fall of 1976, at 21 years old, I said goodbye to my family and friends, and boarded a plane to London, England, where I would live for the next six years.

Mike and I lived in a hotel for three months while we worked on purchasing a house. We had a rental allowance from the company plus expenses for a certain amount of hotel time. That income combined in such a way for us that we were able to purchase rather than rent a house. We bought a modest home on a cul-de-sac in Windsor. I became a homemaker while Mike went off to work. During our first year, I got acquainted with neighbors, became part of a neighborhood ladies coffee clatch, and joined a yoga class. I also lost a lot of weight. The weight loss was intentional but it seemed as though the more weight I lost, the more Mike wanted me to lose. When I fit into one size, he would buy me clothes a size smaller.

I tried finding a church in the area and we went to one for a short while but it didn't last. We had a good-luck doll hanging on our hall wall that we got on our honeymoon in the Bahamas and after I had hosted a church meeting one evening, a deacon in attendance commented on the doll. He said he wouldn't have it hanging in his house. I responded that I wasn't superstitious.

In the Beginning

He rebuffed that it had nothing to do with superstition. I was hurt at his comment and the deep loneliness I had suppressed for a year peaked and overflowed. We did try to find another church but it was easier to just not go, so for the rest of our time in England we never attended.

Not being in the regular fellowship of Christians led to a downward spiral of spiritual discipline and an escalation of everything carnal that lurked inside my young, adventure-some spirit. I still cringed over the way Mike looked at me during our more intimate moments, but I grew hard to other things, like R-rated movies, nudity, and strip clubs. Mike was proud of the way I looked and didn't seem to mind when men saw more of me than they should have. He seemed to enjoy when I dressed provocatively and on vacation he encouraged me to disrobe as he took photos. Sometimes I complied. Other times I refused. While Mike ogled and flaunted my body, other men took notice. My sense of worth diminished with every look.

Our time in England was filled with a lifestyle for which I was completely unprepared but apparently handled well enough for all external appearances. Within a year of our move, I went to work at the same office as Mike. I was promoted quickly. We both traveled frequently with the business, entertained out of town guests, worked at the Paris International Air Show and Farnborough Air Show, and made many trips "across the pond" either for business or home leave which was granted every two years. Vacations were always SCUBA diving trips. We went twice to the Gulf of Aqaba, once to the Cayman Islands, and in 1979 we were part of the first British Diving Expedition to Truk Lagoon in Micronesia.

In January of 1983 we returned to Canada. We bought a beautiful home, resumed church attendance, made some new friends and looked up some old ones. It was so good to be back at church. I got involved in music ministry and began working part time as secretary at two churches. It was wonderful to have regular spiritual input. We lived a few city blocks from Mom and Dad and I visited often. Sunday became family time and life for me, returned to what felt like normal. Then in June of 1984 my father died in his sleep at age 63. It was a devastating shock, but amid the grief was a gratitude that at least we were home for a year and half and had made some lasting memories during that time. I can still see Mom and Dad walking up the pathway to our home, holding fingers. They rarely held hands, but locked fingers as they walked. It was a sweet gesture that is etched in my memory, and still brings me comfort.

Dad was one person who never betrayed the truth of his disapproval of my marrying Mike. We had only one discussion about the matter, which I think Mom likely precipitated. Dad came into the kitchen where I was sitting, and, in his shy, awkward way, just blurted out, "So you're really going to marry this guy?"

My affirmative response was determined and bordering on disrespectful, I'm sure. There were a few more sentences exchanged, and the conversation ended with Dad exclaiming, "You'll have only ten years of marriage," and exiting back into the living room. He died a few days before our ninth anniversary, so when our 15th anniversary rolled around and our marriage was well and truly over, I realized Dad had known all along.

I was 35 years old when I left my husband and returned to the east coast. I had asked Mike for a time of separation. His response was that I could "leave anytime, the sooner the better." I found an apartment in my home town, eventually bought a small house, and applied for teachers' college. I was single, though not yet divorced, a home-owner, and a soon-to-be teacher. I was scared, but I was home and that was what mattered to me. I got called for an admissions interview at the teachers' college just down the road from where I had purchased my home. Everything was falling into place. But much to my surprise and disappointment, I was not accepted into teachers'

college so I sold my house at a loss, and headed to a Christian college in New Brunswick. I graduated with a B.A. in Sociology three years later. The same year I graduated, I learned that my divorce in Ontario had been finalized.

During my education in New Brunswick, I was invited to apprentice in a private counseling practice. The plan was for me to gain a Masters degree in counseling so that I could be in place to carry on the practice when my mentor retired. I applied, and was accepted, to a seminary in Manitoba that offered a well-respected counseling program. It was a rigorous and disciplined two years, but it was filled with personal and professional growth. I graduated in 1996 and once again headed back to the east coast where I would slide seamlessly into my new life in private counseling practice. Or so I thought.

3
THE CALL

It was 1997. I had just received a unanimous call to full-time pastoral ministry. I didn't sign up for this, unless making a deal with God counts as signing up.

It was just over a year before, the summer of 1996. My plans for a career and living in the east had been interrupted when my counseling mentor decided to delay his retirement. Now I was traveling the 2000 miles back to seminary when my car broke down leaving me stranded near a busy city about half way between my starting point and my destination. I pulled to the side of the road and within minutes a police car came by. The officer asked me if I was okay and I told her I was. I have no idea why I didn't ask her to take me into the city since I was stranded well outside of its perimeter. Maybe it had something to do with the fact that I thought the car would miraculously start up again if I just gave it a rest. There was no indication from the dash lights that the car had overheated, or that it was out of gas, or that I needed to "service engine soon." And it hadn't spit out a spark plug as it had gotten in the habit of doing. On those occasions I had wrapped tin foil around the worn plug, turned it back into its housing and prayed it would hold for a few more miles. It always did. I had replaced the rocker cover gasket twice and learned a few tricks about distributor caps and carbon tracks.

For the past year, I had broken into the doxology each time I turned the ignition key in my faithful but tired ten-year old blue Pontiac Sunbird and it had revved to life. Now, on the side of the highway, I needed to think. When I couldn't come up with a solution after trying the ignition key a few times without the doxology, I decided to call for help.

I had no cell phone but I was a licensed amateur radio operator. Another thing, along with SCUBA diving, I had done to fit into my ex-husband's world, and for which I was grateful. That summer, doing a pulpit supply at a Presbyterian church for six weeks, I had met another radio operator who offered to install an antenna in my car for me so my 2-meter radio would actually work. The antenna had broken off when I had navigated a low-ceiling underground parking garage the year before. The use of the radio was a great gift because I was almost always able to connect with a fellow amateur during the long night hours of driving. I was a poor seminary student so stopping before dark to find a hotel room for the night was a rare occurrence.

"VE9-BA. VE9-BA. Anybody around?" I put out three calls before a scratchy response came from an amateur living in the nearby city. Before long a tow truck was on the way with instructions from my new amateur friend to take good care of me. Oh how hard it was for me to relinquish my trusted blue friend into the hands of strangers. Nevertheless I was treated well for no charge. The next thing I knew, a friend of the amateur radio operator with whom I had initially made contact, was picking me up from the towing service to drive me to a hotel owned and operated by his friend, Elizabeth.

Elizabeth booked me into a room in her hotel and told me to get some rest. Barry, the friend who took me to the hotel told me he would be back in the morning so we could go get my car and tow it to Canadian Tire. I sat on the edge of the crisp, clean, hotel room bed thankful to be settled for the night. While I didn't know how I would find money to fix whatever was wrong with my car, I was confident that it would be fixed and I would be on my way at least by later the afternoon of the next day. I couldn't have been more wrong.

Betty Anne Johnson

As promised, Barry arrived early the next morning to take me to get my car from the place to which it had been towed. He hooked a huge tow rope onto my car and to his van and slowly towed me the two miles or so into the city to Canadian Tire's service center. We left my car there after I got a few more of my things from it, and once again, Barry took me back to the hotel. Canadian Tire would call me when the car was ready.

Barry told me he attended one of the local Baptist churches and since it was the weekend, he wanted to know if I would be interested in accompanying him and his wife to church on Sunday evening. I said I would be happy to if I were still in town. I would gladly have gone to church but I never intended to still be around.

Tucked safely back into my hotel room, I made phone calls to family members looking for financial support in case the fix to my car would be more than I could afford. Hearing the familiar family voices weakened my resolve and I found myself crying each time I said goodbye. Here I was, alone, in a strange city, with no money, a broken car, home *1000* miles behind me, and seminary *1000* miles ahead.

A knock came on my hotel room door. It was Elizabeth, bearing a hot homemade meal and fresh baked rolls. I joked about having such wonderful service from a hotel. She stayed and chatted awhile. Elizabeth told me that she had been praying for someone to whom she could minister. She said she checked people in and out of the hotel all day long but because most patrons stayed only one night, she never had a chance to connect with them, to hear their stories, or to encourage them on their way. She had been praying that God would send someone to her for whom she could be a real blessing. Elizabeth also told me that she attended a local Pentecostal church and asked if I would accompany her to church on Sunday morning. I told her I would be happy to if I were still in town. I didn't think for a minute that I would be.

Early that afternoon, I got a call from Canadian Tire. The car was beyond their service center's capability. It needed a whole new engine. I would need to come and get my disabled car off their property right away. I called Barry. He came and got me. Fighting tears, I signed the papers retrieving my car and Barry dutifully towed us to the back parking lot of the hotel. Feeling a lot less confident, and no longer independent, I thanked Barry for all he had done, trying hard to fight even more tears.

I spent the rest of the day walking the streets of the city looking for a tender soul at a car dealership, any car dealership, who would lease or sell me a car. Since I was out of province and a poor student with no credit, there were none to be found.

I returned to my hotel room and began to gather all of the things from my now immovable vehicle. The man at Canadian Tire said the best place for my car was a junk yard. I was crushed. I had bought the car new. I had taken good care of it.

Each trip I made from back parking lot to hotel room, carrying things I thought I needed in my apartment at seminary, weighed my heart further. What could I do now?

Barry stopped by to check on me. I told him I couldn't find a car to lease or buy, mainly because I was from out of province. It was then that he told me he was a mechanic and if I would trust him with my car he would have a look at it and see what he could do with it. He said it might take some time but it wouldn't be any good to me the way it was. The possibility of having my car fixed, lit a fire of hope inside me and I wholeheartedly agreed. What did I have to lose? Of course I would leave my car with him. I could take the bus back to seminary. I didn't know how I would get my car back or how I would pay Barry for fixing it, but at least now I felt some hope. Shortly after Barry left, there was another knock at my door.

I opened the door to a man who was possibly a decade younger than I. He was not a big man. He appeared kind and gentle, but confident. He said he heard that I might need some boxes. He pulled box after box out of his little hatchback car and laid them on the bed in my room. I think the total of his time at my door was likely less than five minutes. I was surprised to say the least. I asked how much I owed him, and he said I owed nothing since I was a "sister in Christ." Before I knew it, he had driven away.

"Hey! Wait! What's your . . . name?"

The Call

I was never to see him again. I later asked Barry and Elizabeth if they knew who the man was who brought the boxes, and neither of them knew. The number of boxes he left with me, and their size, was exactly right to pack up all my belongings for shipment. To this day, I wonder if he was an angel. I know he was an angel to me.

I made reservations to take public transit - the bus - to seminary. It left at midnight on Sunday. Sunday morning I went to church with Elizabeth, packed in the afternoon, and went to church with Barry and Jan in the evening. I also shared my testimony and sang two solos at the church that evening. Then I had sweet fellowship with the friends I had made over the last few days, while enjoying a pizza supper later in the evening. Elizabeth and her husband took me to the bus station where we exchanged hugs like we were old friends, and they prayed for me. How marvelous it was in this difficulty to hold the hands of a brother and sister in Christ and hear their heartfelt prayers on my behalf. I hugged Elizabeth again and thanked her for all she had done for me. As I stepped into the bus, her last words to me were,

"I hope you get a chance to witness to someone!" Little did I know how that someone would change my life forever.

The first part of the bus ride was uneventful. I must have brought a book to read or maybe I just spent the hours looking out the window, I really don't remember. After several hours the bus pulled into a Tim Horton's to give passengers a break. Interestingly, it was the same Tim Horton's that had been my regular stop on the journey from home to school.

He was sitting in front of me. He said he was the relief bus driver. There are always two drivers on board. After we had our break, as I was getting back on the bus, he caught my eye and started the conversation.

"Do you do this trip often?" he said.

"I do actually. But usually I'm in my car. It broke down this trip. This is my first time taking the bus."

I continued to my seat and he turned to continue our conversation.

"Where are you headed?" he asked.

I told him the name of the school and he lowered his head and said he was familiar with it. I asked if he had attended there, to which he said he hadn't, but perhaps he should have. So I asked if he was a born-again Christian and he said he was a "nominal" Christian. We chatted about Christianity and Jesus' love for us, what I was studying at school, and how long he'd been driving buses. The time goes quickly when you're deep in conversation and before I knew it the bus was pulling into a bus terminal where he would get off and I would take a short walk to stretch my legs before resuming my journey. Night had fallen. My conversation with the bus driver was over. Another conversation was about to begin.

I stared out the window at the darkness. I could make out the trees shadowy essence as they disappeared behind us. I reflected on the conversation I had just had, and Elizabeth's parting words,

"I hope you get to witness to someone!"

I began to cry silently. I could feel the moist tears rolling freely down my face.

"Lord, please send someone to reel him in. Please let me see him in heaven someday." The tears wouldn't stop. Then I heard the whisper of God as if it were as audible as the conversation I had just had with my bus driver friend.

"You see, Betty, that's your pastor's heart."

"Okay, Lord, I'll go. But You have to put me there."

I had finally done it. I had surrendered to God in this area, even though there were conditions attached. God had been calling me for over 20 years to serve him in pastoral ministry but for that same 20 years I had been kicking at the goads. Now I had put it in God's hands. If he really wanted me there, it was up to him.

I have prayed the same prayer as I prayed that night for my bus driver friend many, many times over the years since, and today I have the substance of things hoped for. I am confident that I will see my bus driver friend in heaven. It will be nice to know him then, by name.

I don't recommend making deals with God, but it was one of those times when my heart led my head and before I thought twice, I had prayed the vow. All God had to do was take me up on it and there would be no backing out. When God orchestrates the symphony, you play the instrument you've been given.

The first time I felt God calling me to be a pastor was the Fall of 1972. I had always known I would return to the east coast to go to college, after my family moved to central Canada when I was a young girl. I enrolled in college in the east and entered the ministerial program. But it was not so I could become a minister myself. That is, unless it was only to support my husband in ministry, because even though I was in a denomination that ordained women for all levels of leadership, its practice belied its policy. Even ordained women were subordinated to male roles. So I wasn't yet convinced that women in ministry was biblical,

The Call

or at least not what God wanted for me. Women were made for a supporting role and that is what I was determined to do.

In the second year of college, my new roommate was in the business program. We connected, and within several days of returning for my second year at college, I had switched programs, leaving Church History and Introduction to Philosophy behind me in favor of business math, typing, and Gregg shorthand. I graduated that year, 1974.

Ten years later, in 1984, at a Christian camp meeting, I had a spiritual experience where I surrendered myself completely to whatever God wanted for me. Mike was at the camp meeting with me and as was the custom, an altar call was given. This was a time at the end of the service when people were invited to come forward to a kneeling rail which was set aside and dedicated to God as a special place of prayer. When the invitation was given, I felt compelled to go forward. As I stepped out, Mike grabbed my arm to keep me from going. I pulled my arm free and headed up the aisle.

I knew ministry was impossible because of my situation, but during a quiet moment within a few hours after my spiritual renewal, when I was asked by a friend what I thought God wanted me to do, the words I heard coming out of my mouth were, "I believe God wants me in ministry."

The next twelve years would be fraught with tension, tears, and turmoil, resulting in one divorce, two degrees, and three summer pulpit supplies at a Presbyterian church in New Brunswick. I still wasn't convinced as I travelled on the bus in the summer of 1996 that God really, truly wanted women to serve as pastors. In fact, a few years earlier when a friend was being ordained, I prayed fervently the night before that God would prevent her from making such a terrible mistake. He didn't. Now I had made a deal with Almighty God; and if he kept his side of the bargain, I would end up not only being a pastor, but a single one at that. The thought was paralyzing.

"How's the new church going?" I asked my seminary classmate as we took a break from Intermediate Hebrew in the seminary lounge. He lowered his eyes and said,

"Good. But they want an adult Sunday School class in spiritual warfare and I don't have a clue."

My friend was in the ministerial program. I had just graduated from the counseling program. Spiritual Conflict was a required course for counseling students. I said,

"That's easy. I don't have field service this summer. I can come and teach that."

He said, "Great! I'll pick you up Sunday morning at seven!"

"Wait! Don't you want to at least let them know I'm coming?"

"No! I'll pick you up on Sunday. Be ready!"

The Call

And ready, I was. Every Sunday through the spring and summer of 1997 we ministered at the little church just across the border in small town USA. I taught Sunday School. My friend preached the morning message and led the worship service. Occasionally we would sing a duet. Most Sunday afternoons we would go for a drive. Some Sunday afternoons extended well into the evening and we would come north across the border in the wee hours of the morning, having sung every chorus we could think of from our own Sunday School years, as the miles clicked by behind us. They were seminary days, with student loans, papers to write, exams, study, and deadlines to meet, but they were also carefree days of developing lasting friendships, spiritual growth, and wise counsel from well-tenured and caring professors.

As the summer came to a close, my friend and I were invited for dinner to the home of one of the families in the church. The chairman of the church board was at that dinner. We enjoyed great food and conversation and then there was quiet.

Looking at my friend, the chairmen asked, "What are you doing in the Fall?"

My friend explained that he was going to be working for the seminary in admissions and recruiting. He had already accepted the job. I felt every eye turn in my direction.

"What are *your* plans for the Fall, Betty?"

"Whatever the Lord wants me to do!" I exclaimed, and the conversation turned to other matters and the previous lively chatter resumed.

Back in my apartment at seminary, I couldn't shake the question. Sometime that week I called the Chairman and asked what he had in mind when he asked me about mt Fall plans. I asked if he thought the church would ever consider a female pastor. Thinking about the conservative nature of the church where I had ministered for the past five months, I was quite sure this particular church family would not entertain the idea of a woman in the pulpit.

The chairman said, "You mean you?"

I simply said, "Yes." to which he replied,

"Leave it with me."

The next thing I knew, the congregation had voted and unanimously agreed that they wanted me to come to be their next pastor. I had not sent in a resume, formally applied, or candidated. God couldn't have been more obvious if he had written it on a banner in the sky. "Okay, Lord. I'll go. But you have to put me there." There wasn't a doubt in my mind, he had. There would be no turning back.

4
DON'T CRY

Since I wasn't an ordained minister, I could not work in the USA as an R-1 (religious worker), but the paperwork for me to enter the country legally only took two months and in November of 1997 I was able to live and work where I was called to minister. The parsonage, located right beside the church, was beautiful. The furniture was sparse but it was more than many seminary students might have, and the pay was substantial considering I had been living on student loans and part-time jobs for the past seven years. I was looking forward to at least ten years of ministry in this tiny town that was close enough to the Canadian border that I didn't feel too far from home. I was especially excited about leading people to Jesus. With God's help, I would make a difference in this town. I would reach the lowliest of the low. I would open my heart and my home to anyone who had a need. I would pour myself into reaching the lost, and setting an example for these precious people whom I had already come to know and love.

God had been faithful in fulfilling his side of the deal. Isn't it amazing how God works things out for us when we are at least willing to go in his direction? The paralyzing feeling I had when I thought about the deal I had made that night in the bus melted into a passion for ministry and a confidence in the experience I had had, that told me with certainty, God had placed me in this position. And since God never contradicts his own word, the doubts I had about the biblical evidence for women in pastoral roles, also melted into that same passion.

Since I was nervous about preparing sermons every week for the next ten years, I bought two volumes of John Maxwell's sermons. These were bound in two huge binders with CDs of each message being delivered by John Maxwell, himself. For the first few months, I learned to mimic in a female voice, of course, the voice on the CDs. Eventually, I started inserting my own thoughts based on reading the scripture and studying the myriad of commentaries I had accumulated over my years at seminary. It was nice to have the sermons all laid out. I only had to pick the one I would preach each Sunday. It left me free to engage with people and check out the needs in town. My philosophy in those days, was to find the deepest need in the town, and

Don't Cry

then figure out a way to minister to that need. That hasn't changed.

I discovered that this was a town with a great divide. There were those who went to the bar, and those who went to church. And neither those who went to the bar, nor those who went to church, seemed to associate with one another. The need was clear, and the purpose for my call was obvious. Those in the church must reach those in the bar. We must claim this territory for Christ.

Late one afternoon, two ladies from the church and I, made our first bold move. We went to the bar. While one of the ladies engaged the bartender, who happened to be her cousin, in conversation, I walked casually up and down the open area of the bar praying at each table and bar stool, claiming it for Christ. I prayed for the souls who would sit in those spots later that night. I prayed that someone from the bar would come to church so we could extend a welcome and show our love to "the least of these."

As the weeks went by, our congregation grew and we did see a few people come to church who occasionally went to the bar as well. In fact, within the first year, our church family doubled in size. Most were not members, but they claimed our church as their church. We tried new things by way of outreach like having our services for the month of August in the town square. That was a huge success, and one Sunday morning, we even spotted the bartender sitting in a lawn chair out behind the bar listening to the service. We invited the local Sheriff and deputies, Lions Club, and Ambulance workers to a Community Appreciation Service. We provided a gift bag to each worker with the Jesus Film as part of our gift of appreciation, and we fed them a full course turkey dinner served by our young people. As a single woman in ministry, my plate was full and my heart was overflowing with joy.

The more we became visible as a church family, the more we became the topic of conversation in the community. Pretty soon, I began to visit some of the people who didn't frequent the church but did frequent the bar. I got to know them and listened to their stories. They let me pray for them. I felt so positive about all that was happening. God was going to do a great thing in this little town and I was the one he was going to use to make it happen. I went from digging in my heels in prior years to now running full-speed ahead. I was loving life and consumed with reaching out. Eventually, I began to drop into the bar. I would have a soda and talk to the few people who were there since it was usually earlier in the evening when I made my visits. Little did I know I was running headlong into the Red Sea which wasn't going to part with the wave of my hand.

As with anything that grows quickly, there are growing pains. As the church grew, so did the fears of those in the church who loved and appreciated their church family just as it had always been. Those fears turned into doubts about the pastor and her unorthodox ways — visiting the bar and the bar people — it just wasn't proper behavior for a pastor. At the next congregational meeting there would be a larger-than-usual attendance and some tough questions would get asked. There had been some rumblings among the people and a few kind souls had mentioned to me that there might be extra people at the upcoming congregational meeting. I called my friend with whom I had ministered that summer, and asked if he would want to come and give me some support.

Sure enough, the Sunday of the congregational meeting, there was an overflow crowd of members and visitors. The regular business was done quickly and the floor was opened. Someone said they were concerned about the pastor's activities. This person didn't know what the pastor was doing in the evening and felt like she should know that. I was a little amused at that thought, but also irritated. I hadn't answered for my whereabouts for years. This was something new. I wondered if I would actually have to start giving an account of where I had been on any particular day or night. Surely not!

Someone else said they didn't think it was right that I should be visiting with people who didn't go to the church, in other words, the bar people. Since there were several bar people at the meeting, they were careful with their words. This comment created quite a debate between the two sides. As I listened, I became more and more aware of just how great the divide really was in this community, and I also became more angry but especially sad. My friend sensed my emotion, leaned into me and said, "Whatever you do, don't cry!"

His warning jerked me back to the reality of the situation I was witnessing. These were precious, well-intended church members who were fearful of their church's reputation and the breaking down of the long dissociation that was an integral part of their town's culture. Now the barriers were breaking down and it was upsetting. Things would never be the same. Here in the church, both sides were present, and both sides were arguing. And I thought to myself, "Well, this is good. At least they're talking."

As I came out of my thoughts and back to the conversation, someone was questioning whether anyone really knew what it was I was drinking when I was at the bar.

Someone stood and yelled, "Excuse me, I know what she drinks! Diet Coke." Silence reigned and someone else quietly asked a bit sarcastically,

"How can you possibly know that?"

"I'm the bartender," came the response.

When all was said and done, I had agreed not to go to the bar again unless accompanied by a church member. That was not a problem for me, except for the spontaneity of my prior visits. Now, I would need to be more deliberate about those occasions if there were to be any. Truly, I felt it would be better if I just never went back in the bar again. I was discouraged and felt shamed for trying to do something that I thought was a good thing.

My friend had kept quiet through the entire meeting, but just as it seemed to come to a standstill, he stood and explained that even though he hadn't intended to say anything because he was just there to lend me some support, he felt it was important for the church to decide if it would stay as it was or reach out into the community. With his words of wisdom, and gentle applause from several in the room, the general consensus seemed to be that the two sides should at least make an effort to get along.

I wondered what had changed inside of me because of the meeting. I felt a little lost. I felt like perhaps the people I had come to serve had not been served well. And yet the people who seemed most likely to never attend the church where I was the pastor were standing up for me. They had actually come to this meeting, perhaps at first, just out of curiosity, but in the end they were the ones who were the most vocal in my defense. Something didn't seem right. I was confused. And even though my friend had also put in the effort to travel a distance to show his support, I felt strangely alone. I wondered what was ahead for me as a pastor in the town. And whatever it was, would I have to stand alone?

5
THE FALL

It was well into the second year of my ministry and my people and I had settled into a comfortable routine of concerts, prayer walks, outside services, and community outreach including praying for the whole town. Each church member was given ten names from the phone book to pray for. Whether business or individual, everyone in our small town would be brought to God in prayer every week. Some people prayed for their ten daily.

The divide between those who frequented the bar and those who frequented church appeared to have softened considerably and a level of trust between pastor and people developed in the wake of the lively discussion from the year before. The church continued to grow. I still had a deep sense of loneliness even though I felt a keen awareness of purpose in what I was doing.

We had a good group of young people who interacted with other youth in town. My Confirmation Class rallied with other youth for baseball games and activities we held. I was still adjusting to balancing ministry passion with expected behaviors but for the most part, pastor and church family were growing and developing what appeared to be a strong and healthy relationship. Reaching out into the community came in different formats now. I had discovered other avenues of service which I thought would be just as effective, if not more so.

A new pastor came to a church in the town south of us. He was interested in starting a Law Enforcement Chaplaincy program in the county. We met at the monthly ministerial meeting where he spoke of his interest. The other pastors appeared less responsive to the idea, but after the meeting, Erik and I talked at length about the possibilities. We were hooked. We took classes from the State Police's Chaplaincy program and gained the hours we needed to become State certified Chaplains. We developed a descriptive and procedural manual, raised funds for uniforms and necessary accessories. We approached the county sheriff who was open to the idea and instituted it almost immediately. We were put on a schedule of ride-alongs with the Sheriff's Deputies and called on to help with death notifications, inmate transfers, and any other assistance the Sheriff might deem necessary.

Law Enforcement Chaplaincy was a good way to serve the community. It motivated me to look for other ways in which I could serve without being a solo act. It wasn't long before I discovered something I had always been interested in and never taken the opportunity to do. I enrolled in a course to become an Emergency Medical Technician - Basic.

Being an EMT was extremely rewarding and allowed me to meet many members of the community and beyond. In addition to the Basic course, I took the extra hours to certify as an ambulance driver. Since I did not live in the town where the ambulance shed was located, when there was a local call, I acted as a first responder, assessing the situation, taking vitals, and administering oxygen as needed. Coupling the EMT work with Law Enforcement Chaplaincy proved to be worthwhile and exhilarating. When responding to a vehicle accident as a Chaplain, I could still keep an eye out for injuries, take vitals, and administer help where I could until the ambulance arrived. When responding to a call as an EMT, I could, if asked, provide pastoral care.

I loved what I was doing. The church was flourishing and I was helping people in all types of situations. Better yet, one of the deputies' duties was to make bar-checks. During ride-alongs, those bar-checks included me. When my pager went off for an EMT call, the trouble sometimes was at the local bar. It was a win-win combination.

Betty Anne Johnson

I don't remember how, or when, we met. He was new in town and it was a very small town, so it was inevitable that we would meet eventually. At some point, we discovered our mutual interest in the game of Scrabble. He often made his way the short distance from his home to mine, where we would spend the evening playing Scrabble and trying to "cheat" by using foreign but "real" words. We talked for hours, and somewhere during those conversations, we became more than "just friends."

I sat at my desk in the church office a very troubled soul. I had been happily celibate for ten years. Questions reeled through my mind. How could I have let this happen? What did I need to do? Could I ignore this one incident and never let it happen again? I had already confessed my sin and felt God's forgiveness, but I felt I had let my people down, which I had. I felt like the purity with which I had come to this place was now gone. What would or should happen to me? The anxiety of the moment was unbelievable. Where do I turn? What do I do? Who do I tell? Anybody? While I was steeped in my anxious, guilt-ridden thoughts, the phone rang.

"Hello, Betty. How are you doing?"

"Fine. Thanks. How are you?"

The Fall

"I'm well." The conversation was brief and cordial. Finally, he said, "I just wanted to call and see how things are going there and check in with you."

"Thank you. That's nice. Goodbye."

"Goodbye, Betty." Click.

I was stunned. This was my pastor-to-pastors. He was supposed to check in more often than he did, but the timing was certainly no coincidence. I knew why he had called. God was giving me the opportunity to confess. I made another deal with God.

"If he calls back again, I won't hold back, Lord. I promise, I will confess."

There was no possible way he would call again. Why would he? There was no reason. The phone rang.

"Betty, I wanted to mention to you . . . pause . . . Betty, are you okay? How can I help?"

The details of what followed are a bit of a blur but I confessed my sexual sin to him. He told me not to mention this to anyone else but that eventually I would have to tell the pastor who served over all the pastors in the area. This person is referred to across denominations as the District Superintendent, Regional Superintendent, Regional Minister, Area Minister, or Bishop. Since I can't remember what he was called in this specific denomination, I'll call him the Regional Minister. The pastor-to-pastors suggested that the coming Saturday might provide that opportunity. It was a conference in another town where local pastors and church members would gather. He also told me that if I wanted him to preach on the coming Sunday, he was available, and would be willing to do so.

I was shaking when we hung up and my thoughts were racing faster. Only this time it was that I had even confessed, and would have to confess yet again. What have I done? Why didn't I just keep my mouth shut? What about *him*? What will happen if this all gets out? Strangely, I never entertained the idea that I might lose my ministry.

Then as if a lightening bolt hit me, I heard the beautiful promise of 1 John 1:9:

If we confess our sins, he is faithful and just to forgive us our sins and to cleanse us from all unrighteousness.

I felt at peace. I knew I would be okay. This is how the church operates. We confess our sin to one another and receive forgiveness. I opened my Bible, pulled a couple of commentaries off the shelf, and began to work on Sunday's message. I also picked up the phone and made a counseling appointment.

In the days that followed I shared my story with a few of my friends who had no connection with my church or its denomination. After carefully listening to my plight, one friend said his philosophy was, "private sins, private confession, public sins, public confession." I liked what he said and wished that I had followed his logic during the week immediately past. When I expressed my anger at myself to another friend, exclaiming, "I've been happily celibate for ten years!"

He said, "Well now you've been happily celibate for ten years less a day."

That kind of encouragement, helped bring perspective to my situation. While I was still very anxious about the future, I expected that after possibly very difficult but good discussion with the denomination, a plan would be in place which would not only hold me accountable, but would ease the loneliness and help me grow spiritually and as a new leader.

I went to the conference on Saturday with three church members. Toward the end of the day, I saw the Regional Minister. He was sitting at the back, by himself, so I knew it was time. I asked if I could speak to him and found an empty room in the large church. We sat at a table in what appeared to be a Sunday School room. I confessed my sin to him. My expectations were that he would offer forgiveness, ask me what boundaries I had set in place so that it wouldn't happen again, pray with me, and perhaps require me to meet with one or more female pastors who would ask hard questions but also provide a source of strength and encouragement for the journey I was on. His first words after I had given to him what seemed to me like the whole story and assured him that I had confessed my sin even as I was doing again now, were:

"How did it happen?" I was shocked. Just exactly what was he asking? We were both adults. We know how these things happen, don't we? At that moment, I felt like I was sitting with a voyeur who was using my vulnerability to satisfy his thirst for power. In reality, in his own ineptness, he may have asked the question to determine if I was a victim. In that case, the question could have been much more direct and specific. I did my best, while trying to maintain some self-respect to tell this man the basic, but more specific details of our indiscretion. It was the most uncomfortable, degrading, disrespected, and shamed feeling I can ever remember.

Looking back on that hour in that Sunday School room, I realize that if this man had had my best interests at heart, and if he had asked the question about how it happened in order to determine if I had been victimized in any way, then he would have realized his mistake as soon as I began my response. He would have stopped me immediately, and clarified the question. Instead, he listened stoically and when I finally finished, he offered no words of comfort or concern, only a sterile outline of the next steps.

He would be approaching the ministerial board to see what would need to take place. In the meantime, I was told again to speak to no one of my situation, especially no one in the church.

The Fall

He also did not offer to pray with me nor did he ask if I had sought forgiveness from God. He did not inquire as to any steps I might have already taken in terms of boundaries in regard to my opposite-sex relationships. He stood and left the room saying he, or someone from the denomination, would be in touch.

I sat for a short time and reflected on what had just happened. I did not want to leave the room. I did not want anyone to see me. I felt naked and ashamed. I was scared. I was wounded. Nevertheless, the conference was over and there were three dearly loved church members waiting for me to take them home. All three took one look at me and were filled with compassion and concern. I told them I was not allowed to say anything but yes, something was going on, and yes, I wished with all my heart I could talk to them about it, but I must obey the rules, and I was told not to speak of it. They asked no further questions, said they would pray, and all three said they were available whenever I was allowed to talk. The drive home was quieter than usual but still filled with moments of chatter about the conference.

When we arrived home, I called the pastor-to-pastors and told him if it wasn't too late, I would be most grateful if he would preach for me the next day. He was ready and willing, and assured me of his love and support in whatever may lie ahead.

Betty Anne Johnson

The following week I was called to a meeting at a hotel in a city north of the border. I was allowed to bring a friend for support and one denominational advocate. The pastor-to-pastors who had preached for me the previous Sunday offered to act as my advocate and since I didn't know a whole lot of people in the denomination, and he and his wife had been so supportive, I readily accepted his offer. The friend who would sit with me was a friend from my counseling program at seminary. We had kept in touch after graduation. We had visited one another and shared our secrets and dreams for the future.

The room where we met was the small sitting room of a hotel suite. Two chairs sat in the middle of the room facing a small sofa and another chair was beside a small table against the same wall as the room's entry door. My friend and I were invited to sit on the sofa. Three men sat in the chairs facing us. The men comprised my advocate, the Regional Minister, and the Executive Minister from the ministerial board. The seating arrangement meant that the only women in the room were positioned lower than the men.

On the table in front of the sofa was a small tape recorder. I was told that the meeting would be taped. I was uncomfortable with that but I didn't say anything. Looking back now, I realize how naive I was. The questions began and lasted for just under two hours. I can't remember any of the questions I was asked. I believe now it is because I was traumatized. My friend told me later that every time the Regional Minister asked me a question, I squeezed her hand tighter. After the meeting was over, I was given the opportunity to ask questions. I asked if I could now talk about this to others. They told me I could now talk to whomever I wanted. They also told me that I would be hearing from them and the tape recording would be kept on file and after a specific period of time, it would be destroyed. I cringed at the thought of the tape being held somewhere "on file." The meeting was over.

    My friend and I said our goodbyes. The pastor-to-pastors' wife was waiting for us in the hotel lobby. She could not attend the meeting. She and her husband asked me to join them for a meal on our way home since we were all heading south. I told them I would like that and we went on our way.

    As I drove south toward the restaurant, I realized this thing had gotten bigger than I ever expected it would. I still held out hope that my confession counted for something. I still hoped that when the ministerial board met, they would at least hear my heart since they didn't know me. I felt particularly encouraged that the worst was over and now I could talk to my people. I wanted desperately to tell my church family what was going on. I knew the ones who had gone to the conference with me were very concerned for their pastor. They had checked on me several times during the week but without a hint of wanting to know more than I could tell them, and assured me of their prayers.

I remember eating together with my advocate and his wife, but again, I don't remember any of the conversation, other than one thing. My advocate had not spoken during the two-hour meeting. Now he was suggesting to me that he felt my discipline would be lessened if I had not actually had intercourse. His not-so-subtle inquiry felt very different than the questions of the last two hours. He was looking for a way out for me. He was still searching for a way of escape from what he knew might be ahead, even though I was still completely oblivious to it. At that moment I was given the chance to change my story.

I could have said, "Oh no! It wasn't like that at all! We just went a little too far, that's all! We didn't actually . . . " But I wasn't going to compromise myself again. That would just add insult to injury. If I was going to continue in God's grace, I needed to continue in my integrity. I remember the heart-felt prayer he prayed on my behalf before we left the restaurant that day. Tears flowed freely from us all as we embraced and said our goodbyes. Not only was I oblivious to what lay ahead, I didn't realize the worst wasn't yet over.

6
GUILT AND GRACE

The first person I called when I got home was a church board member. She and I had become close friends. I trusted her completely. She was one of the three of us who had done the initial prayer visit at the local bar. We had been on prayer walks together. She lived in grace and was kind and caring. If I had been allowed to talk to people in the church, she would have been my choice as a friend to have at the meeting from which I had just come. She had also been with me to the conference the previous week.

I told her my plight and we cried and prayed together. I asked for her forgiveness and she offered it graciously and with the assurance of her love always. This began a series of visits and phone calls: first, to the church board who also offered their love and forgiveness and their assurance that they wanted me to continue as their pastor. Every church member was either visited or called. For most visits, I was accompanied by one or two other ladies who were church members. In every case there was grace and mercy extended to a broken and contrite pastor. Comments were varied -everything from the suggestion of marriage, to the idea that it was nobody's business but mine, and that I had to have a life too.

That Sunday, only the second week after my confession (though it seemed like a lifetime), was filled with incredible love and support. The church pianist played, "Marvelous Grace" as part of her prelude and told me later it was for me. When I had confessed to her, she had admitted how hard it had been for her to remain chaste during her single years. Several asked if I had heard yet from the denomination. I had not. Most just wanted to know that I was okay. It can be difficult for church members to view their pastor as a sexual being, and part of the fallen human race requiring God's forgiveness and mercy.

It would be almost a week before I would hear from the denomination. It seemed to me that the call would come on a weekday since it was the denominational office. On Saturday morning, however, when I least expected it, the phone rang.

The Executive Minister was very blunt. He advised me that I would need to "step back" from ministry for one year. He did not suggest what would fill that year (in terms of restoration), when

Guilt and Grace

that year would begin, or how the denomination would step in to help the church during that year. I cringed at what I was hearing. I had never even considered that this would be my penalty. I was heart-broken and could not understand exactly what he expected. Was I to not even go to the church the following day? What does "step back" mean? Did they want me to surrender my license? Through my shock I told the Executive Minister that the church people wanted me to stay on as their pastor and that they had forgiven me and offered their grace and mercy. He sounded angry (or at least frustrated) asserting that it would not be possible unless there was a 100% vote of the church.

I called the church chairman and gave him the details of my conversation with the Executive Minister. I was devastated. I didn't know how, or where, I would move. I was in the country for this purpose and this purpose alone. Would I be given time to pack my things? Would I find a job before the money ran out? I had furnished the parsonage from its meager beginnings and was truly settled. This was my home now. I spent the rest of the day in a haze.

That night, I crawled into bed and buried my head in the pillow. What was I going to do? I felt a darkness come over me like I had never experienced before. I thought, "So this is what people feel like before they commit suicide." It seemed the only way out. Just then, my dog, Charlie, a Bichon Frise, moved from the bottom of the bed where he usually slept, to cuddle in close to my head. I heard the Holy Spirit say to me, "Betty, you have options. You always have options." Charlie's movement and the whisper of the Spirit shook me out of my darkness. I had options. I might not know what they were right then but there were options. Darkness no longer overtook me, but a peaceful sleep.

Sunday morning, I came to church to find the Chairman of the Board already there. I always came to the church quite early so it was unusual to find anyone there at that hour. He told me he wanted some time at the end of the service. Compared to the week before, this Sunday was much harder. The verdict was in. I felt so uncertain about my future. Would this be the last time I would see these precious people as their pastor? Looking back, it's hard to believe that I was so fearful during those tenuous days, but loneliness can be debilitating and I had felt for a long time as if I were flying on my own. Even with new-found church friends, a lovely home in which to live, and a flourishing ministry, I felt a foreboding loneliness. Now, on this Sunday, my home and native land felt like 2000 miles away rather than only 20.

At the end of the service the church board chairman told the congregation what the Executive Minister said to me. He said they needed a 100% vote in favor of my staying on at the church. I felt compelled to interject that it was only if they really wanted to vote that way! The chairman again emphasized the importance of a 100% vote. The vote was taken and it was 100% in favor of my continuing as their pastor. I was relieved and surprised. Any one person in this congregation could have made the entire difference and everything would have changed. Instead, every ballot confirmed, at least at some level, that this church family not only forgave me, but continued to see me as their pastor. Now it was time to inform the denomination.

On Monday, several members of the church board met in the church office with me to draft a letter to the denomination. We decided, as an act of submission, that we would surrender my denominational license and the local church, within their prerogative to do so, would issue me a license or ordination certificate.

In addition to the official letter from the church to the denomination, I included a letter I had written outlining what I perceived to be the abuses of the process to which I had just been subjected. Both letters were perceived as "rebellious" even though that denomination held that the local church is autonomous and makes its own decisions regarding the call of pastors and staff.

The reason I wrote specifically about the abuses I felt I had incurred, was because at a denominational meeting earlier in the year, pastors were shown a video of things to avoid in dealing with young people. The video outlined abuses which can happen even when they are not intended. Every nuance highlighted in that video as abuse, had just happened to me as an adult, perpetrated by the same denomination. While I did not assert myself in the process that I had just undergone, I was certainly aware that the methodology employed, however unintentional, was seriously abusive.

Because of the outcome of the disciplinary action initiated by my confession, there was very little interaction with the denomination in the coming months. The Executive Minister had warned that a congregation does not "get over" this kind of sin for at least ten years. Neither the church nor its pastor believed his statement, although the months and years ahead would prove just how fragile we really were. Whether that woundedness came from the disciplinary process or the sin itself will likely never be known this side of heaven.

In the month that followed, the Regional Minister of the denomination called the Christian college where I was teaching a sociology course to freshman students. He apprised him of my status with the denomination. I received a call from the college president who assured me that since it was late in the school year, and since I had confessed, I should plan to finish out the year. I thanked him as graciously as I knew how but was extremely angry that the Regional Minister had done such a thing. I didn't know if it would have been considered ethical or not. It felt very unethical to me. I wondered if it was even legal. I was pleased that once again, however, I had experienced grace.

At the end of the week that the president and I had had such a positive phone conversation, I received a message that – he wanted to see me in his office at my class break. The visit to the president's office proved to be opposite of our phone conversation. I was not to return to class and was dismissed immediately. When I questioned our phone conversation, the president's words were, "I cannot make a unilateral decision like that." Those are the only words I remember from our meeting that day. I left the president's office and went straight to the professor's office for whom I was teaching. I told him my story. He went and dismissed my class for me and stayed with me until I was able to retrieve my things from my office. He walked me to my car, and I headed south to my little town where I knew there was a community of grace.

How news travelled in those days, I had no idea. As usual, I arrived at the next monthly ministers' meeting for the denomination. I felt we had followed denominational protocol and since I was still serving one of their churches, it seemed logical to me that I should continue attending the ministerial meetings. These were my brothers in Christ. I was the only female pastor in that region. These men of God received me into their fellowship from the first meeting and I wasn't going to let my sin define me, or prevent me from being the best pastor I could be.

Betty Anne Johnson

When I arrived at the meeting, I was greeted warmly and since I had arrived just on time, the meeting started right away. The pastor who was leading our time together read Galatians 6:1 and admonished his brothers that they all were right on the edge at any time of being exactly where I was that day. For a few minutes I received words of encouragement and affirmation from my spiritual brothers and we had a blessed time of prayer together. The meeting then turned to the matters and conversation that was normal for our gatherings. We enjoyed coffee and stories and, most of all, grace.

Months passed and the church continued to flourish. Our growth spurt stabilized in favor of a gentler increase in our church family. Occasionally there would be a reminder of our woundedness, like the not-so-secret little giggles of a couple of young people at our community activities where both I and my gentleman friend were present. There was some negative feedback in the form of letters from church members suggesting that my chaplaincy work was only so I could be in the company of male officers. There was a heightened level of scrutiny concerning my whereabouts. Any single female pastor who has lived in a small town has likely endured some level of curiosity as to the motives for her actions. Nevertheless, I continued my ministry and the chaplaincy and EMT work until the wounds began to openly fester and bleed.

Guilt and Grace

The tenure of a pastor is usually quite short compared to other occupations. Another new pastor had arrived at the denominational church in the town north of where I was serving. I sent him a note of welcome and invited him to our monthly ministerial meetings. I assumed he felt warmed by my gesture as he called and invited me to have coffee with him and his wife early one morning. I said I would be delighted and arrived promptly at the specified hour. As I entered the house, it was clearly in chaos. The children were rushing to get to school and the pastor's wife was busying herself with household kitchen chores and children. The pastor was in the process of pouring coffee, reached for another cup and poured me one as well. He asked me to sit at the table which I did. The children were rushed out the door. We talked for just a few minutes. I asked about his children as I tried to relax in the chaotic atmosphere. His wife continued to busy herself at the kitchen counter. For some reason I felt uncomfortable, and only a minute later, I realized why. The pastor gulped his coffee, looked at his watch, and with that gesture, I stood to go. He said they needed to get going as well, but said he wanted to confirm that I was the pastor who had the affair. He had heard about it from the denominational office. I said something about it not being an affair, said it was nice to meet him, and left as quickly as I could. All together, I was maybe in their home for ten minutes. On the drive home, I realized to some extent at least, just how fresh my personal wounds still were. I also pondered that if this is how things played themselves out in these kinds of situations, then perhaps the Executive Minister was right about the ten years to recovery.

My first experience with denominational discipline took me from gullible and naive to eyes wide open. I know I can still be pretty credulous at times. I like to see the very best in people so I tend to assume they will most often respond with grace and mercy, especially when their response is in my direction! I've discovered that people generally live out of guilt or grace. This makes a world of difference as to how they respond in all kinds of situations. I've also discovered in talking to colleagues and peers associated with various denominations, that many, if not most, Christian denominations operate from a guilt-based system for their ministerial accountability and discipline/restoration process. Perhaps this is because, in most cases, pastors get caught rather than confess. I firmly believe 1 John 1:9, *If we confess our sins, he is faithful and just to forgive us our sins and to cleanse us from all unrighteousness.* This verse tells us that God cleanses us from all unrighteousness, not some, not just certain bits, but *all* our unrighteousness, and we all have plenty!

It would be fool-hardy to suggest that 1 John 1:9 means there should be no consequences for a sin confessed. All discipline, however, needs to fit the person being disciplined, to help that individual minimize the chances of repeating the same sin. I would contend that some denominations deal with sins rather than people. Dealing with the sin rather than the sinner, leads to disposing of the problem with the least amount of damage to the system. It is the proverbial tail's wagging of the dog. If a pastor is caught or confesses to a certain sin, there are matching disciplines regardless of the pastor's track record, self-administered disciplines, or the consensus of the local church. These all, however, should be taken into account in any disciplinary action. A relational process for discipline is exceedingly more difficult.

As Christians, we are called to confession. A community of grace is the longing of the Christian's heart and it is only in a community of grace that a believer truly thrives and grows. We are called to confess our sins to one another that we may receive healing (James 5:16). Churches and individuals continue to flounder with festering wounds because confession is not a natural outflow of their new life in Christ. The Spirit is quenched just as surely as confession is quenched for fear of the policies which have punishment at their root rather than grace.

7
ARRESTED!

Beyond the abuse inflicted at the hand of the denomination, the damage my sin caused to the trust of my congregation and the wounds of my own soul, combined to provide ripe soil for the enemy's insatiable desire to devour all that is good in God's kingdom. It took some time, but before very long, a few of the precious souls who had offered their pastor a vote of confidence the year before, were now wishing they could vote her out. It seemed as if every move I made was under the scrutiny of a certain few in the church family. An incident in the context of my chaplaincy work would lead to serious doubts about me with the people I most wanted to reach for Christ—those who frequented the bar more than the church.

Arrested!

One evening I was preparing to go to the sheriff's department as part of my regularly scheduled chaplaincy work. As I drove out of my yard, I heard fireworks and thought it was coming from just a block away on the street with both of the town's bars. It sounded like fun, so I went to say hello and to maybe see a few minutes of the fireworks. Any time I noticed the slightest opportunity to make a connection with the town people, I tried to do it. This was just such an opportunity, and I could make this connection without having to go into the bar. I stopped by, said hello to a few there in the small gathering and went on my way. As I turned from the town onto the highway, I noticed a squad car turning into town. I thought nothing of it, waved, and carried on.

I put in a good night of chaplaincy with no major incidents and came home as I usually did at about midnight, feeling purposeful and content. I noticed the light on my answering machine was flashing. The message came from someone who had been in the small gathering of people who were lighting fireworks. It was a nasty message which included name-calling and threats accusing me of "telling the cops" about the fireworks. The interesting thing was that I didn't even know that setting off fireworks without a permit was illegal! That squad car I had seen earlier in the evening had appeared at the scene and put a stop to the fireworks fun. I was immediately and irrevocably suspect. Still, I felt that I was making inroads with at least a few of the people in town who so desperately needed Jesus and I would not stop fighting on their behalf.

Reaching people who have been ousted by well-meaning Christians takes a lot of time and patience. I had built relationships of various kinds with several of the people in town. One dear lady I called my "over-the-counter" friend because we only saw each other in the mornings when I came to get my cappuccino at the gas station where she worked. I became very close friends with our female mail carrier. She wasn't a church-goer but was open to discussing spiritual matters and we truly enjoyed each other's company. Another girlfriend was a functioning alcoholic who had a heart of gold.

It wasn't the female friends I had outside the church who were dangerous ground, but the males. I had as many male friends in college and seminary as I did female friends. In-context, with Christian brothers and sisters, it works. Elsewhere, it is a field full of landmines. In order to help one male alcoholic friend, I spent hours with him drinking coffee and playing cards. It kept him out of the bar. One evening he showed me a bag of white stuff he'd been given or bought. With his permission, I flushed it down the toilet. If he ever had any more, he didn't tell me about it. On another occasion, he arrived at my door saying he needed to pray. I took him over to the church where we knelt down at the front of the church and he prayed out of his heart's longings. His sister and mother visited me one day to express their astonishment and gratitude for the change they had seen in him.

Not everything I tried was as encouraging. One male alcoholic rang my doorbell in the wee hours of a winter morning. He claimed he had nowhere to stay and it was cold. I showed him to the guest room and left him to himself. In the morning he was gone but in his alcoholic haze he had mistaken the guest room floor for the bathroom. Several months later, the doorbell rang again in the early morning. Whoever it was rang the bell persistently and I could hear an inebriated male voice but it was warm outside. I buried my head under the covers and resisted the urge to extend hospitality. I was either getting wiser or losing my heart of compassion, I didn't know which.

Brewing in the church at that time was an underground cauldron of discontent. As is quite often the case, it wasn't clear what the specific issues were. The church board members were supportive and kept me accountable. They also let me know when there was gossip in town — that is, when they knew. One such story was sad and hilarious at the same time. The story was that two brothers in town were fighting over my affections. Both gentlemen were alcoholics and both had been on my doorstep more than once. During one conversation, as I was leaving the house, one of the men said he loved me. I appreciated the sentiment and never once took it to mean anything other than a love that I was open to talking with him and helping where I could. Unfortunately, the neighbor overheard that part of the conversation and, likely as a result of the gossip, honestly believed it to be a mutual expression of affection. When a board member told me what had happened, it gave a whole new meaning to Ephesians 4:29 to let your conversation be an encouragement to those who may happen to overhear!

Being a single woman in ministry can be daunting and funny all at once. Some of the visitors we had during my four-year tenure were simply there to "check out" the new single woman pastor. Even church members couldn't avoid suggesting now and then that this one, or that one, would make a great match for their pastor. Before long, however, the yeast of mistrust that was festering with a few of them would rise to a crescendo for which even the church board was unprepared.

A small group of discontented church members, after over a year of denominational estrangement, wrote to the Regional Minister requesting his help in "taking back their church." The Regional Minister was most agreeable to the group and met with them without prior knowledge of other members of the church, including the church board. A formal meeting of the church was called by the Regional Minister but without the board's knowledge or consent. It became aware when a member, on the Saturday before the meeting, mentioned it, not realizing that they had not been notified.

Despite the unprecedented nature of the meeting, it went forward with the minimum number of members needed for a quorum. The Regional Minister presided over the meeting. Several members, including board, boycotted the meeting as unconstitutional. I was voted out by a narrow margin effective immediately. I decided it was best that I go. With the support of the board, I was granted severance pay and several weeks of vacation that was due me. The actions of the Regional Minister left the church and especially the church board, in a state of confusion. He had come and gone, given this small group of members what they wanted, and left the church as a whole high and dry and divided.

Several members who felt that they were the true church since they had abided by the constitution, decided simply to relocate. I led their services for three weeks and then encouraged them to return and reconcile with their discontented brothers and sisters. Some did. Others left in favor of attending nearby churches. One member who did not leave the church had worked at one time as an ancillary worker at the border.

During my weeks of vacation I was busy looking for another church to serve. I was offered a position in a church in Canada which seemed like the perfect opportunity. I didn't know how I could afford to move there even with the calling church's help, but I did ask the church for a couple of days to think about their call and to pray about it. The more I prayed and the more I wanted to go, the more I heard the Spirit telling me to stay where I was. With tons of hesitation and a heart full of fear and doubts, I told the church in Canada that I couldn't come. They sent an email expressing their disappointment but support for my decision. I too, was disappointed, and didn't give myself much support for my decision other than I thought that was what God was telling me to do.

In the final weeks of my vacation, all packed and ready to move somewhere, but not knowing where, a knock came to my door. It was one of the sheriff's deputies. I assumed there must be a chaplaincy issue when he told me there was someone outside who wanted to talk to me. I walked to the driveway where the squad car was parked. Standing beside it was someone I had never seen before, but I recognized the uniform; he was a border control officer. He told me he was placing me under arrest for being in the country illegally. I was horrified, terrified, and shocked. I argued with him! He was polite and told me he had received a report from the church that I was no longer the pastor and therefore was illegally in the country. I told him I was on my vacation so that technically I was still the pastor. I asked him to please go in and talk to the people who were in the church to clarify it since they were meeting there at that very time. He wouldn't do it. When I knew I was going to have to go with him, I asked if I could change. He gave me time to go back in the house, pack some things, and change my clothes. I called my friend on the board and she came immediately to the house. She tried to plead my case but was unsuccessful. The deputy was the one whom I had only done a ride-along with once. When I told him how important it was for women who are abused to talk about it, his body language showed discomfort and he said he knew about abuse but he'd never heard it talked about so openly before. That night, something in me wondered if he might be an abuser. The night I was arrested, that suspicion became palpable.

I was told I should follow the officer to the sheriff's office where I would be booked. I followed obediently. When we arrived at the station, the border officer and I walked well in front of the deputy who was trailing. The officer told me in a quiet voice that he would make it as easy on me as he could. As we walked into the place that had once been an inviting partnership, the dispatcher on duty raised his eyebrows in a sympathetic gesture. I was finger-printed, had my arrest picture taken, and was asked to sign a confession by choosing one of three statements none of which applied to me. I was told that if I didn't pick one, I would stay in a cell overnight and would need to talk to my lawyer the next day. I was informed it would "take a long time." If I signed, I would be taken to the border and "released" into Canada. I chose an option and signed the paper in disbelief at how confining and unjust the so-called justice system can be.

Betty Anne Johnson

Once the paper was signed, I thought we would be on our way to the border but the deputy then reminded the officer of my EMT work. I had noticed that the officer away from the presence of the deputy, seemed to be more kind and caring. In the presence of the deputy he raised his voice and used harsher words and gestures. He told me that I was not allowed to do EMT work. I told him that it was volunteer. The deputy interjected that I still got paid for responding to a call. What could I say? And if I was being deported, why would it matter anyway? I could sense the pleasure the deputy took in seeing me in such an awkward and uncomfortable situation. A few years later, I had the opportunity to meet and talk with his wife. If ever a woman had been a victim of abuse, she had.

Before long, I was once again dutifully following the officer to the border. While we drove in tandem, I called my friend to keep her up to date on what was happening. She was praying and trying to get through to the church's board to see what was going on. As we headed toward the border, I had hoped that it would be closed. It always closed at ten p.m. but I didn't know in this case if someone would be waiting to let us through, or if this was just an oversight on the part of the border officer. If it was closed, it would give my friend more time to find out what was going on and try to stop it if that was even possible. I also called friends of mine just north of border asking them if I could stay with them for the night. I told them what was happening and they assured me of their prayers and their hospitality even though it would no doubt be an absurd hour of the night or morning before I would arrive.

The border was closed. I pulled up behind the officer. He came to my car window and told me that I would need to follow him over to the 24/7 border crossing. We turned and headed in the other direction. I called my friend and updated her. She said she was still trying to get some answers. Once we arrived at the second border crossing, it was close to midnight. The officer gave the border guard some papers and the phone rang. The guard excused himself and went to answer the phone. He looked up at us and said,

"Yes, they're here right now. Okay. Okay." He pulled the phone over to the officer who had arrested me.

"Yes. Okay," said the officer.

He hung up, picked up the papers he had laid on the counter, and told both the border guard that we were turning around. We stopped at the USA border office where I was given a six-month visitor visa.

God is in all things. He was in the timing of getting to the border and he was in all that happened the most terrifying night of my life. By 2 a.m. I was snuggled safely in my bed. I learned that my friend, in desperation, had called another board member, gone to the chairman of the board's house at about 11 p.m. and demanded that he call the border to get things resolved.

Betty Anne Johnson

Several in the town had heard what had happened by the time I got back, and my dear non-churchgoing girlfriend was waiting up for me to make sure I was okay when I finally arrived home. I went from panic to peace in seven hours — but they were very long hours!

The parsonage never looked so good to me as it did the night I was arrested and turned around at the border. Even with that horrible experience, not knowing what was going to happen to me, or to all my things, I still felt God wanted me to stay stateside. Why? I had no idea. I was safely in the USA for six months, but I had to soon move out of the parsonage. I simply had no idea where I would be going.

One of my non-church girlfriends, had been looking at the classifieds daily on my behalf. One evening after work, she knocked excitedly at my door. I welcomed her in but not before she waved a piece of newspaper in front of me saying she'd found a great job for me! She was right. It would be a great job . . . if I could get it. I applied for the position as an Outreach Social Worker in a county south of where I was. I was pleasantly surprised to be called for an interview. Three days after the interview I received a letter of employment. Because I had a B.A. in Sociology, and because I would be employed as a Social Worker,

Arrested!

I was able to turn in my visitor's visa in favor of a work permit under NAFTA.

Now that I had a job, and was back in the USA legally, I needed a place to live. I looked at several apartments, but decided to purchase a cozy trailer house in the city where I would be working. I made final preparations for the big move. I still didn't know, though, what on earth I was doing still living in the USA.

8
ICE CREAM

With the purchase of my new trailer house I sent out a plea for my friends to help me move from the parsonage. On moving day there was a convoy of cars and pickups at the parsonage door. The loading began and it didn't take long before everything was out of the parsonage and put rather precariously in the trailer house on the sales lot where it sat. I had bought the house new and it couldn't be moved until the next day but the seller graciously allowed me to move my things into the house prior to them hauling it to the trailer park. The trailer park was one of the nicer ones in town with mostly newer mobile homes and more mature residents. My house had a unique shape to it with an angled front which allowed for a huge window in the eat-in kitchen. There was a nice-sized master bedroom, another small second bedroom and an adequate living room. It was more than enough room for one person. I used the smaller room for extras and within a week was nicely unpacked and living the dream in my cozy home with my new job. My colleagues at Social Services were welcoming and I loved my work. The pay was good and the hours were somewhat flexible which was great because there was a lot of traveling involved with the job of making unannounced visits to clients' homes.

Even though I received good wages, my financial situation became strained with the addition of a mortgage and utilities to pay. I was determined not to lose my house, so over the winter I sold all of the furniture I had acquired during my four years of ministry. With the coming of Spring, despite sleeping on an air mattress and having a futon as a sofa, I was content. I was happy in my little house, and I enjoyed my job. There was a longing however, to be back in ministry of some sort so I started to look for opportunities. Since I could not offer myself even as a licensed minister, I looked for ministries in para-church organizations. One particularly caught my attention and I had a phone interview with them. It was to be a house parent in an orphanage in Massachusetts. Now, though, it felt more like I was looking for a job to survive, rather than the excitement of a specifically God-ordained calling. I was thinking about the possibilities when I heard a loud noise outside like someone might have lost their muffler.

Betty Anne Johnson

It was a Sunday afternoon, and I was sitting in my kitchen when I heard the noise. To my surprise, nobody had lost a muffler! Two motorcycles were pulling into my driveway. It was Ron and his friend, Tim. They had been two of the many who had helped me move from the parsonage late in the summer the previous year. Tim was single and had never attended my church. Ron was separated and, while not a regular attender, had come on several occasions. I was pleasantly surprised to have visitors on a sunny Sunday afternoon.

Tim and Ron asked me if I wanted to go for a motorcycle ride. This would be a new adventure for me since I'd never been on a motorcycle before. I was a little wary of people trying to set me up with eligible bachelors so once I got ready and went outside, I deliberately headed for Ron's bike since I thought he might be trying to match me with Tim. It was, I'm sure, quite a hilarious sight. Since I had never ridden a bike before, I didn't know how to get on one. I tried getting on rump first. I planted my rear end on the seat but knew immediately that it wasn't going to work. Why those two men didn't burst out in uncontrolled laughter is beyond me, but they were kind, and Ron suggested I try hopping up onto the left peg and swinging my right leg over the passenger seat to the right side of the bike. I tried. It worked! All settled in, Ron got on the bike and told me I could secure myself by holding his shoulders or by putting my arms around his waist. I put my hands on his shoulders, but I felt so comfortable on the bike, I didn't even feel like I needed to hang onto anything.

    The men started off cautiously. I could see Tim keeping his eye on me to make sure I was okay. Once we got to the open road, he eased his bike behind Ron's bike and to the right of the lane. I was learning the proper ride formation and didn't even know it. What I did know was that I absolutely loved this experience. The wind was exhilarating and there was something about it that made me completely relax. I felt like I didn't have a care in the world. Ron leaned back and yelled to me,

"Are you sure you've never ridden before?"

"No! Why??"

"You're a natural."

    I wasn't sure what he meant by that but I did know that I was enjoying this new adventure immensely. I wanted to go forever. It was the most fun I had had in years. We rode to a local casino, walked around a little bit, then headed back the way we came.

    When Tim and Ron dropped me off, I couldn't remember when I had felt so good. I was hoping they would say they would come back again and they did! The next Sunday they came again, and the next Saturday, and then again, and again. One evening Ron came by himself and said he'd like to take me out to dinner. I thought that was so nice of him. Remember, I'm rather naive. We enjoyed dinner at a local restaurant and he brought me home. Still, it was the ride to and from the restaurant that highlighted the evening. I felt like I would do almost anything if it meant getting a motorcycle ride. I was definitely hooked. Whenever Ron and Tim showed up, I was more than ready to hop on the bike and take off for a ride.

After our dinner, Ron occasionally called me at work. We had become good friends and I certainly enjoyed his company. Then one day he called and said he and a few of his friends were going for a ride the following Saturday. I was so disappointed. I knew that meant he wasn't coming to my place. Then he asked if I would like to go with him and his friends. I don't know if he was able to finish his sentence before I said a very determined, "Yes!" The sense of disappointment I had felt a few seconds before told me that I was attracted not just to the motorcycle, but to its rider.

When people today ask us how we got together, we both agree it was the ice cream sandwich. While we were on that first ride with his friends, we stopped for gas. I stayed with the bike and Ron went inside to pay. When he came out, he was eating an ice cream sandwich and he had one for me as well. I took the ice cream but started to cry. Ron was afraid he had done something wrong, but I assured him everything was fine. As we continued on our journey, I explained to him that my first husband never bought me ice cream. He was always very conscious of my weight and restricted my diet to ensure that I remained within the weight limits he felt were best for me. To have a guy actually buy me ice cream without my even asking triggered an emotional response that Ron least expected and for which I was unprepared. It gave us the opportunity though, to have a candid conversation about our pasts. It would be the first of many candid conversations. Three months later we were married.

9
MOVING ON

Sometimes, just when you think something is over and done with, that's when it rears its ugly head again. Ron and I had been married only a month or two. I sold my cozy little trailer house to a nursing student. There wasn't much to move since I had already sold the bulk of my furniture. Still, since Ron had even less furniture, my meagre additions made a huge difference to the spacious farmhouse. Some major cleaning and considerable patching and painting, and we were nicely settled. Then one night we got an unexpected knock at our door.

Ron opened the door, surprised to find his ex-wife looking composed, but angry. She came in and told us that the church had just had a meeting to try to respond to charges against their current pastor. The charges were not unlike the ones I had faced. They seemed to me, however, to be more humiliating. The same Regional Minister as when I served the church still held his position in the area and was at the meeting. He apparently made mention of the former pastor breaking up a marriage. When he made the statement, he didn't realize to whom he was speaking among the crowd. A lady stood up immediately, informed the Regional Minister of her identity and stated categorically that no such "break up" as he put it had taken place. She added that she did not appreciate what had just been said about her family since it was not true and it bore no relevance to the current situation. That dear lady was Ron's first wife. She had come to let us know what happened. She thought we'd want to know.

That night, Ron made a phone call to the Regional Minister's office. He left a voice mail message strongly encouraging the Regional Minister to cease and desist, or bear the consequences.

Life on the farm was another unique experience for me. I was a townie. The farmland was rented out, but there was still plenty of work to be done on the homestead. Ron's farm had been established in 1880, so it had the distinction of being a Century Farm, even though Ron's family had never applied for the official designation and the accompanying sign. But being a Century Farm was a big deal in the Midwest. The family farm was a valued and treasured heritage, one not to be taken lightly. Previous generations had worked hard to provide a living for those following. Father handed to son, who handed to his son. Farm families were known for their hard work and by the number of sections they farmed. They were, and still are, considered pillars in the community.

The homestead consisted of five acres of property, with farmhouse, out buildings, a barn, a pole barn, and a large shop (garage). Mowing the five acres took one full evening if we started right after supper and both of us worked at it. I -used the rider mower, and Ron did the push mowing around the edge of the woods and buildings. Many times, Ron's friend since childhood, Tim, would come to the farm and help with mowing ditches, or work on a project Ron had underway on farm equipment or motorcycles. In the winter, the heated shop was full of bikes lovingly bedded down for the season. It was always a joy to have Tim at the farm. He was a good friend, a gentleman, with a kind and tender-hearted spirit. He was also a strong and capable farmer. But Tim wasn't the only visitor to the farm.

Hunting season always coincided with my birthday, November 2. Ron and I were married October 12. That meant deer hunting came within the first month of our being husband and wife. I was still getting used to Ron's kind of country living. He never locked the doors to his house because, "What if somebody needs a place to crash for the night?" I was confused. Didn't people have homes of their own where they could crash? After our talk about locking doors, I assumed Ron began the nightly practice that in my way of thinking was the natural thing for the man to do — secure the house for the night. Early one Saturday morning right around my birthday, I thought I heard noises downstairs. It wasn't unusual for us to have a mouse or two in the enclosed porch but I thought the sounds I was hearing were a little too deliberate for a tiny rodent. I pulled the covers gently away from me and as quietly as I could, I got out of bed and left the bedroom. I walked carefully down the hall. I was still hearing noises. It sounded like someone was in the kitchen. I crept halfway down the stairs, just far enough to peer over the railing and down the hall to the kitchen. There in the shadows I spied a very tall figure wearing a long black duster. I was terrified. I flew back up the stairs, jumped into bed, punched Ron on the arm, and in as loud a whisper as I could muster, said,

"Ron! Get up! Get up! There's someone in the kitchen!"

Ron turned, tiredly looked at me like I had two heads, pulled the covers tighter around him and said,

"It's okay. It's just Marlin."

Just Marlin! There was a tall guy in my kitchen at 5:30 on a Saturday morning who I didn't even know was coming! I must admit, he was quiet for such a big guy. I snuggled back into bed but since Marlin had arrived, Ron knew it must be about time to head to the woods. That was the morning I learned that Ron's house became the "hunting shack" every November. And I learned that Ron often forgot things — like warning me that a tall dark stranger might invade my kitchen on a Saturday morning in November! I also learned that Marlin was a gentle giant and a good friend.

Pretty soon I could hear shots being fired so close to home I wondered if I should take cover in the basement. They weren't actually that close. It was just that this was all a new experience for me. By mid-morning there were three skinned and gutted deer hanging from the front-loader in the yard. Another new experience for me and not one of which I was very pleased. Ron did promise they wouldn't butcher and wrap their winter meat in the kitchen, which apparently was standard practice. I was grateful. The unpleasant part of deer hunting gave way to the joy of guys, like fishermen, sharing their stories and talking about the one that got away. I tried to be a good host even though I felt completely clumsy at it. But at least I survived my first hunting season.

We had another visitor who came in the winter. It was two o'clock on a frosty morning and we heard a loud rumble in the yard outside. Ron and I both awakened and sat up to listen. In the quiet of that frigid morning, we heard Hagar (his nickname) yelling to us from down below.

"Hey! You got any booze?!!!"

Ron was a recent recovering alcoholic, so it wasn't unusual for people to think that he might have alcohol in the house. But apart from the bottle of brandy for winter colds, we didn't have any. What was unusual, at least to ordinary folk, was that Hagar was on a four-wheeler in the middle of winter. He had already had 16 DUIs so his only mode of transportation was a four-wheeler. What was also unusual about this visit, was that Buddy (his nickname) was somehow hanging onto the back of the four-wheeler. What wasn't unusual was that both men were completely intoxicated. I decided it was my turn to pull the covers tightly around me and let Ron handle this one. He went down to the door and told the guys he really didn't have any "booze" in the house. It took some convincing but eventually Hagar and Buddy took off, we assumed to find another unsuspecting neighbor who might be kind enough, or tired enough, to keep their party going.

The summer after we eloped, Ron and I went on two one-week vacations. The second vacation was meant as our honeymoon. For the first trip we were joined by a biker friend. It was great fun to travel together on the bikes. We were headed to Hot Springs, South Dakota, where we would pitch our tents and take in the sights of the Black Hills. I had never been to the Black

Hills so I had no idea what to expect. It was very hot. I got sunburned. I saw more motorcycles than I'd ever seen in my life. I learned up close and personal that buffalo are dangerous. I waded into water where you could move a foot or two from where you were and be standing over a warm plume of water, thus the name Hot Springs. I discovered there are no bugs in the Black Hills. And much to my delight, I also discovered that my allergies didn't bother me at all. It was amazing to feel the freedom of inhaling deeply without pulling for breath.

Our honeymoon vacation was booked along the north shore of Lake Superior. The beautiful landscape of the area makes it a prime spot for everything from luxurious resorts to primitive camping. Once again we loaded up the saddle bags of the bike and our little pull-behind trailer. The sound of the bike idling signaled to me that Ron was almost ready to go. I pulled on my little white canvas shoes, no biker boots for this biker chick, and hopped on the back of the bike like the old pro that I had become. We got to the end of our country road but instead of turning left, Ron hesitated. He turned around to ask me a critical question.

"Which way? Left to Duluth, or right, back to the Black Hills?"

We both grinned and then broke into huge smiles. Ron revved the six cylinders of the Valkyrie, and turned right. Our honeymoon had begun.

Moving On

Summer turned to Fall and another Winter on the farm set in. Ron and I talked a lot about our future. Ron talked about living in the Black Hills. I talked about living in Nova Scotia. Wherever we went, we decided it was time to move off the farm and make a new life for ourselves. When the Winter finally yielded to Spring, and Summer rolled in on its heels, we had an auction sale, pitched a tent in the local state park and prepared to head to South Dakota. Ron had taken a quick trip there a month before the auction to scout out a potential new home for us. I had my name in for a church in Nova Scotia but hadn't heard anything. We decided if we hadn't heard, that would be sign enough that we weren't supposed to head east, and we would instead, set our sights on South Dakota. We both enjoyed the area; that much we knew from our two trips there the previous summer.

We got a better confirmation than just hearing nothing. We heard, through a phone call with my mother, that another pastor had been offered and accepted the position. That meant we were South Dakota bound. We had a refurbished old truck with a brand new cargo trailer hitched behind it. I would drive our car. Everything we owned was packed in the truck. The cargo trailer was reserved for one Honda Valkyrie motorcycle and one Yamaha 650 motorcycle with a side-car rig attached. We said our goodbyes to family and friends, and the next morning headed south to our new life. Little did we know that one phone call was about to change everything.

Because of the heat of the summer, we stopped regularly to check the tires on the truck to make sure they weren't overheating. During one of our pit stops, we both praised God for His watchful eye over us. We were sure the tires would be blistering hot and we would have to wait a while for them to cool down. But the tires were not at all overheated. Another little confirmation that we were doing the right thing. Before the next pit stop, I would have a cell phone conversation with my mother. She was disappointed, as could be expected, that we were not moving to the east coast. She had longed for years to have all her children living closer to her. I assured Mom of our love but said we needed to head to South Dakota. Still, I gave Ron her message that she wanted to talk to him at our next stop, and he called her. I did not get involved, or interfere in any way with the conversation even though I listened intently to one side of the exchange. By the time the phone call was finished with a mother-in-law my husband had yet to meet, we were turning around and heading for a different new life. This time on the other side of the Canadian border.

Despite having all our earthly belongings with us, the time at the border crossing was relatively quick and easy. It was July 1, and the Border Officer looked at Ron and said,

"Welcome to Canada."

Now all we had to worry about was if the old truck would make it twice as far to the east coast as it was to the Black Hills, and if the hitch on that same old truck would manage to haul its precious cargo up and down the huge hills that lay ahead.

When we stopped for breaks, I learned bits and pieces of the conversation Ron had with Mom. She had promised him that there would be no problem with me finding a church to serve in Nova Scotia. I wasn't as confident as Mom but as soon as we arrived we were offered the chance to visit with the search committee of a two-point parish not far from where my mother and step-father lived. After our interview, we were confident that this opportunity would not be a good fit for us. The search committee agreed and before we called them, they contacted us to say they would be continuing their search.

Disappointed that the potential for a well-paying job was not as readily available as he had hoped, Ron felt that the best thing for us to do was head back to American soil. The truck was still packed. Ron at least had the chance to meet my family. And we had been able to attend my sister's ordination, which was an absolute joy for me but terrified my poor husband. All the black suits and the many people walking around with a Bible tucked under their arm led Ron to think he had landed into some kind of cult. Ordination day was a totally new experience for him and all he could think of was what on earth had he gotten himself into now! His perspective on the day was enlightening, to say the least. Isn't it wonderfully ironic that just four years later, his wish would be to be baptized at that very same campground?

Perhaps it was the fear of that ordination day, or the immediate interview with a search committee, that led Ron to want to run back to the familiar. Whatever it was, it didn't take long before we were westward bound and once again hoping the truck would hold together, and the hitch would hold on. I was devastated. I cried all the way to Pennsylvania where, because of a heavy rain and a nice hotel pool, we decided to stay an extra day. During that day, I had phone calls with my mother and sister. I learned that the pastor of my mother's church had just resigned. My sister intended to apply for the position and I asked her if she would be willing to let me apply instead. She graciously, and without hesitation, released the opportunity to me. I talked to Ron about it but he was determined to stay on course so the next morning we were once again westbound.

We had installed CB radios in our vehicles so we could keep in touch. We only had one cell phone between the two of us. A few miles into the day's journey, Ron radioed me with a question and I returned a clipped and emotional response. Either God was working on him, or he felt as if he was headed for a life of misery with a disgruntled wife, but within a few minutes, he radioed again with a question, I didn't hesitate to answer.

"Do you want to turn around?"

"Yes."

We found a safe place to turn the big rig and our westbound trip turned into an eastbound journey. My spirit lifted. We were going to give it one more try. The search committee would be meeting the following evening so we had to arrive within two short days. Once again Ron navigated the old truck and new trailer up and down the steep hills of the eastern seaboard. I had called ahead to U.S. Customs to see what we would face there having imported, exported and now wanting to re-import our belongings. Fortunately, it was not an issue and once again, the border crossing was relatively smooth and stress-free.

I arrived at the church just as the last member of the search committee was getting out of her car to go into the meeting. I introduced myself, handed her my resume and headed for my parents home where we would stay. I was expecting to find Ron already there. Several miles before, I had stopped for coffee while Ron continued on. Imagine my surprise when I pulled in the driveway and didn't see the big 52-foot all white truck and trailer parked there. Mom and my step-father, Ralph, said Ron hadn't been there and they hadn't heard from him. Needless to say I was more than just a little worried. Ron should have arrived at least several minutes, if not an hour or more, before me. Just as my stomach fluttered with concern and I was about to hit the panic button, I heard a low rumble outside. Much to my relief, a long, slow streak of white shadowed the house. It was the most beautiful sight I had seen in quite some time. Poor Ron! On the road leading to town, which was a proverbial long and winding road, he heard a loud kaboom. A back tire had blown on the truck and he was limping the big rig home on three of its four back tires. It is a mystery to this day why I didn't see him as I came into town on the only road that accesses it. Now, here we were again in Nova Scotia. This time, I thought, "I'm home for good."

10

INTERLUDE

    With all the traveling we had been doing, we didn't have much chance to ride our motorcycles. Now, feeling a little more settled, Ron and I decided to go for a ride. This was the first time Mom and Ralph had seen Ron and me on bikes —Ron on his huge Honda Valkyrie and me on a Yamaha 650 with a Velorex side car attached. Mom took a picture of us and off we went. We rode to the next town where there was a beautiful park overlooking the ocean. We stopped for lunch at a wonderful little cafe and bakery. It was a perfect day. We decided to spend the afternoon cruising the roads, possibly ending up at a beach or an ocean lookout somewhere. Ron was leading the way and I was feeling more comfortable on my bike. I passed Ron and waved, enjoying every glorious minute with the wind in my face. Life was good. We passed a sign announcing the little hamlet of Larry's River just ahead. The next sign announced a curve in the road. Reduce speed to 50 kph. I checked my speed — 50 right on. Only problem was, I was going 50 miles per hour, not kilometers per hour.

It was the most beautiful, peaceful feeling I've ever had in my life. I was flying through the air. I could see the grass slowly coming toward me and I knew I was going to float right through the grass and on into heaven. I have never had such an incredible experience before or since. Then, my dear guardian angel must have heard God say, "It's not her time," and I hit the ground with a thud. A couple of short gasping breaths and I cried out, "Honey! Honey!" Not that he would have heard me of course, but we do and say strange things in these situations. My sidecar had lifted sending me careening off a cliff, landing me on my stomach just shy of the Atlantic ocean. My bike was a tangled mess in the water beside me. While I was a stone's throw off the Atlantic, I was also just a yard or two from a light pole. The possibilities of this being a fatal crash were endless, but God has our days numbered, and my number was not up just yet. Suddenly, I saw another beautiful sight, harness style biker boots straddling my helmeted head.

"Where are you going now?" was all he could think to ask.

"My leg! My leg!" I cried. He yanked my leg out from where it had somehow gotten tangled into a handlebar which caused me

Interlude

to automatically roll over. Now I was on my back. The first thing I did was wiggle my toes. Lying there, I felt no pain. Two men watched the accident from their back deck and called 911. The younger of the two men said he had called the ambulance and it should arrive in about 45 minutes. A crowd began to gather at the top of the hill. Despite his training, Ron pulled my helmet off. By the time help arrived, I was very glad he had.

Firemen arrived on the scene first and positioned me on a backboard. Someone from the crowd said my arm looked weird. My right arm was twisted backwards and positioned too far above my head. One of the firemen took charge of my arm. He slowly and carefully edged it down by my side and put my hand into the pocket of my jeans. That was very painful. I don't know how many fire fighters there were. It seemed like they completely surrounded the backboard. One fireman attempted to put a cervical collar on me. This is where I became most grateful Ron had removed my helmet. They only had a large collar, and the poor man didn't know which way was up. Fortunately, I was able to tell him which way to put it on, and even as efficiently as he did that, the largeness of it caused my neck to stretch and become quite uncomfortable. I heard, "One! Two! Three!" and I was airborne once again but this time on a backboard and in the capable arms of several firefighters. I heard myself encouraging them as they hoisted me up the cliff. "Go, go, go, go, . . . ahhh, good job!" I said as they gently set me down on the side of the road as the crowd made way. I heard them chuckle. It seemed like within a minute of the men getting me to the top of the cliff the ambulance arrived. I was heading to the hospital with sirens blaring and lights flashing. My dear husband of a little over a year was heading to my folks' place to give the in-laws he had just met a few days earlier some serious news. Despite my coherence, he was sure, given the nature of the accident, I had internal injuries which would be fatal and he would be single again.

I was assessed at the local hospital, had my dislocated right arm wrapped a little more securely, and reloaded in the ambulance to head for the nearest city hospital. Interestingly, the doctor who assessed my injuries and ordered me to a larger hospital had been having lunch when Ron and I arrived at that little cafe/bakery a few hours earlier. As she watched us arrive, she looked at my side car and thought she would love to have a ride in it. Ironically, if she had been in the side car when I took that Larry's River curve at 50 miles an hour, the chances of the side car lifting as it did, would have been considerably reduced, and the accident might never have happened at all!

At the city hospital, Mom, Ralph and Ron waited nervously as I went through a battery of tests to determine internal and spinal injuries. Ron wasn't used to the lack of privacy of the Canadian health system's wards, and was most unimpressed when the man in the bed next to me expired and he was left ly-

Interlude

ing there rather than being whisked away from living patients. Ron was also still quite sure that I was going to follow the man in the next bed. He was still certain that I had multiple internal injuries that would within a few hours or days at the most, take my life. I remember Mom, Ralph, and Ron standing by my bedside, but I don't remember anything that was going on around me or even what the ward looked like. I do very clearly remember, however, the doctor coming in, crossing his arms in a sweeping motion one over the other and announcing I had no spinal injuries so the cervical collar could be removed. Oh my, I was glad to get that thing off! This hospital, however, couldn't conclusively determine internal injuries, so once again I was loaded into an ambulance, and this time was on my way to a Halifax hospital with Ron riding shotgun. By then I had been given a few good doses of morphine and according to Ron my greatest concern was that my bike was okay. I needed it in order to keep riding.

At the Halifax hospital Ron was relieved to hear that I had no internal injuries. One left leg very badly broken below the knee with an avulsed kneecap, a seriously dislocated right elbow meaning the tendons had been stretched about as far as the elastic would allow them, and other minor fractures in my right hand which would heal nicely, were my only injuries. I would be wheelchair bound for about six weeks given that my right arm and left leg were out of commission. The cast on my leg was from ankle to thigh. The cast on my arm was from wrist to shoulder. I was a strange looking sight, but I learned very quickly how kind people can be when you're in a wheelchair. I also learned to deeply appreciate push buttons that open doors, disabled bathrooms in the mall, and low sinks that allow for a wheelchair to be pulled up tight to them. Ron took me to the mall a few times when I was in the wheelchair and what a joy it was to wash my hands under running water and to sit on a real toilet and flush afterwards!

At home — that is, in the old country house where Mom and Ralph lived — I was relegated to the living room. During my four-day hospital stay, Mom and Ralph had managed to set up a single bed in the living room which would become my home for the next several weeks. Beside the bed was a commode that I could reach from the bed. Every single intimate detail was taken care of by my dear husband. He put the toothpaste on my brush. He washed and combed my hair. Washing my hair was fun for me but not so much for Ron. I laid on the bed with my head out over the foot of it. He took a wash basin full of water to wash and then rinse my hair and wrap it in a towel. Many trips to and from the kitchen sink were required for this exercise. Mom and Ralph's only washroom was upstairs so he made plenty of trips up and down those stairs as well. He emptied my commode, helped me get dressed, took me for walks, and guarded my dignity every day, 24 hours a day. This was the stuff of love. We just didn't expect it to happen within our first two years of marriage.

Sometime during those early weeks of my convalescence, the search committee asked me to candidate. Ron and Ralph devised a make shift ramp to get me on the platform of the church and I preached my first message from a wheelchair. Immediately following the service, a vote was taken and I was asked to become the new pastor at the Baptist church in the little town of Guysborough. I accepted the call with the only condition being that immigration matters would all work out. We had no reason to believe they wouldn't.

After a few weeks of living with my parents, we were anxious to move into the parsonage and start unpacking. We had been living out of our suitcases for several weeks and Ron still had to care for all my needs. The parsonage was one story so lent itself better to my convalescence. The day came when the house was ready for us and we moved in immediately. I unpacked what I could from the boxes Ron brought to me, but for the most part, he did all the unpacking and setting up of our home. The parsonage was a lovely three-bedroom bungalow, furnished. We just had to add our personal effects. One of the bedrooms in the parsonage was designated as the church office. While it was convenient for work, it was definitely awkward for living. There was a lovely loft in the church which would lend itself nicely to a church office. With me in a wheelchair, however, that solution was out of the question at least for a while. It wasn't unusual for a deacon or some other church official or member to arrive at the house needing to make copies or take care of some other type of business such as filing or retrieving information from the files. One Sunday, a church member asked Ron to visit a single woman who had been to church a few times, who had a wayward son whom she felt could be positively influenced by Ron's presence. Ron was less than enthused about visiting a single mother so he procrastinated as best he could hoping I would soon be mobile enough to make the visit myself.

Two weeks after my accident, I returned to the Halifax hospital to have my arm cast removed and some follow up on my injuries. Four weeks later my leg cast would be removed. And by the time we were eight weeks from my accident, I had graduated from wheelchair to walker to a cane. The following Sunday would be my first Sunday to preach from the pulpit in a standing position. I was excited.

Before that Sunday arrived however, we got word from the USA that if we stayed any longer in Canada, I would loose my green card and my social security. We weren't all that concerned about my green card at the time, mainly because we didn't understand the implications of abandoning it, but I had worked

Interlude

stateside for six years and had made a considerable investment to social security even though I was just shy of the points needed to be vested. Ron talked to me about returning. I wanted to at least stay where we were for the winter months. We were settled. It was the end of September. Why not give it a chance? Then one night, as I slept fitfully, I heard the strangest sound. It was a sound like something being torn apart over and over again.

Rather than being torn apart, I discovered when I fully woke the next morning that the tearing sound I heard was actually packing tape pulling off the roll putting together those boxes we had unpacked only two months earlier. It was Friday. Thursday night Ron had packed all our belongings back into the old truck. We were leaving. I confirmed our departure with the church deacons whom I had alerted earlier in the week. I was heartbroken. Ron didn't know or understand the protocol of clergy departures, and it was too late to try to make it right. I read my resignation to the church Sunday morning and told them we were leaving that afternoon. I have no idea how they felt, but I do know that it was one of the hardest things I've ever done in my life. Not only because I personally wanted to stay at least for the winter, but also because that morning my mother had been admitted to the hospital with pneumonia.

I still cry at the memory of saying goodbye to my mother in the hospital early that Sunday afternoon. She was trying so hard to fight her own tears and I can only imagine how heartbroken she must have been after she had worked so hard and been so happy to have her daughter living in the same town. Like Ron, three months earlier, wondering if he had fallen into some kind of cult, I'm sure Mom wondered who this man was who was willing to drag me away after so much had been invested in getting us to where we were. We had imported our vehicles, changed our licenses, and registered for health care. Now we were running for the border again. But this time there would be no turning back.

After four days on the road, we arrived in the city where I lived before Ron and I got married. We thought there would be good opportunities for jobs and since it was familiar, we booked into a hotel and started our search. We also looked for a place to live. I could see that Ron was grateful to be back in familiar territory but I also recognized that his friends were not as excited about his return as he thought they would be. Oh, they were pleased to hear from him, and to know he was in the area, but I had the distinct impression that Ron was hoping for more of a homecoming celebration. My suspicions were confirmed when he got off the phone with one friend, and suggested the same thing. In fairness to our friends in the area, they were never

Interlude

quite sure what we were going to do next, so it shouldn't have been all that surprising that they met our return with reserve.

While I was sad to have left Nova Scotia and was constantly thinking about my family and the church, it was exciting to be house-hunting, and in the meantime to have a pool-side room in a nice hotel as our only home. There was laundry to do of course, but there were no meals to prepare, a swim every evening, and someone else to make the bed and clean the room. It was easy to get used to the life style!

Within a few weeks, the mobile home we bought was moved onto a lot on the same street where I had lived before. We furnished it and got settled in quite quickly so we could begin our job search. Ron found a job right away. It would take me a little longer. While I was searching for a job, I was also looking for a denomination which supported women in ministry and where I would fit well theologically. I didn't give the strict denomination of my growing up years a second thought. While they supported women in ministry, I didn't believe I would be accepted to a leadership role with them since both Ron and I had been divorced. It would be January when I found a job, and by the time spring was in the air, I found a denomination that I believed would be the perfect place for me to serve.

I was accepted with American Baptist Churches USA (ABC) which placed me on their roster of available ministers. In August, I received a letter in the mail asking about my interest in serving as a pastor in a small town in the Sandhills of Nebraska. I was more than ready to explore the possibility, so on Oct. 2, 2005 Ron and I made our way to Nebraska where I preached, the congregation voted, and two weeks later we were once again packed and on the move. Here, Ron would cut his teeth on the rigors of being a pastor's spouse. He would also take giant leaps forward in his spiritual walk; and that growth would come from a most unexpected source.

11
GENTLE LOVE

We were warmly welcomed to our new church just two weeks after our initial call. The pastor's office was beautiful, overlooking the newly constructed large church entrance. The parsonage was small with no off-street parking but it accommodated us well enough, and it seemed that after only a few weeks, we were completely settled and into a regular routine. Several of the local pastors stopped by to welcome me. Ron found a job at the local lumber yard and made friends easily. I was happily immersed in getting acquainted with the church family and the community. One of the most striking characteristics of the area was the friendliness of its people. Another outstanding aspect was the unique air quality. The city was home to two feed lots, one with 80,000 cows, the other with 20,000 cows. There were no clotheslines anywhere. Ron and I noticed more people there had portable oxygen than we'd ever seen before. But the friendliness of the community and its entrepreneurial spirit was more than enough to balance the unique air quality and no-one seemed to mind it a bit.

Ron and I used our free time exploring the area on our bikes. My bike and sidecar rig that were totaled in the accident, had been replaced with a wonderful little white Honda Rebel 250 that I outfitted myself with bags and accessories. During my hiatus from work, I had finally taken the motorcycle safety course and passed my riding test. Ron was quite happy to buy me a new bike and I felt safer on two wheels than I did on three! It was great fun for us to ride together on our own bikes and Ron even said he was impressed with how well I handled my bike. We were truly enjoying where we were.

One morning, about six months into our time in Nebraska, Ron turned to get out of bed to prepare for work. Except something happened and he couldn't move. He fell back onto the bed in a locked position. He had put his back out. I helped him get to a seated position on the bed and called the chiropractor's office. They would see him right away. He was sent to the hospital for x-rays and learned that he had slipped a disk, but that to complicate matters he had degenerative disk disease. The doctor told him he could forget about riding bike. We found the walker I had used when I had my accident and Ron used it for what little moving around he did for the next several weeks. He also took the doctor's advice and sold his bike. I asked him to sell my bike too since I didn't want to ride without him. He had to give up his job at the lumber yard, as well. Slowly, and after considerable therapy and hard work, Ron graduated to using a cane, and eventually could walk again on his own. He was determined to be better!

Not one to sit around doing nothing, as soon as Ron could, he was on the move. One of his favorite things to do now that he was out of work, was to have breakfast at McDonald's. He enjoyed the chatter of the retirees who came most mornings for coffee. During one such breakfast a man introduced himself as the mayor of town commenting that he noticed Ron might be new in the area. Ron explained who he was and as they talked for a few minutes, the mayor learned of Ron's farming background. He asked him if he would be interested in a job with the City. When Ron said he might be, the mayor said he could expect a visit from the Supervisor of the Parks and Recreation Department. The mayor wasn't kidding.

That afternoon, there was a knock on the parsonage door and the Supervisor of Parks and Recreation introduced himself, talked to Ron, and offered him the job that was to become Ron's dream job. The City boasted seven parks which needed to be mowed and maintained and an Olympic-sized swimming pool. Ron was responsible for mowing and upkeep of these recreational areas plus anything else that might need to be done. He was thrilled with his new job. He rode his bicycle to work, came home for lunch which most days I had prepared for us, and which we sat on the front porch to eat. God was so good to provide this job for Ron. It was easy on his back and also allowed him the quiet time while working (similar to farming) that he so enjoyed. He wasn't at his job for very long when he learned that his boss was a Christian and attended one of the churches in town. He invited Ron to their men's Thursday night Bible study. From that Thursday night until the day we left the church, Ron enjoyed their mentoring and fellowship. That relationship would not only strengthen Ron for a few of the immediate friends we would make, but also equip him with the grace and courage he would need for the journey further ahead.

There were blessings beyond measure with this little congregation in Nebraska. They were excited about the possibility of my ordination. I had only to complete the two required specifically Baptist courses, write an ordination paper, be examined by the ordination council, and be recommended. I had no trouble completing the courses and the date for my ordination council was set.

One of the best blessings for me was outside of the church. I facilitated a Bible study at the county jail. As many as six men might be at the study any given week. Four of the men were regulars as they waited for trial or served their sentence locally. Another huge blessing was the opportunity to provide radio devotions one week at a time with other pastors in the area. Several of those pastors were female clergy, which added tighter friendship and fellowship to the blessing.

We had some interesting interactions during our time in Nebraska. Our first night there, Ron and I were out walking in the cool of the evening and we happened upon a young man who struck up a conversation with us. He seemed very personable, but when he heard I was the new pastor in town, he got quite animated. This young man, we'll call him Brian, was passionate in his belief that Santa was Satan. He also believed that Christians have no reason to have any physical aids, for example, glasses, or hearing aids. He strongly encouraged Ron, in the name of Jesus, to throw off his glasses and crush them under foot. Apart from anything else, Ron is quite blind without his glasses and was reluctant to follow the young man's suggestion. Our dear friend, Brian, attended church off an on and we were always pleased to have him with us. It became a little more concerning the day I found a beheaded doll next to the entrance of the church and the police ascertained that it was Brian's mischief.

Betty Anne Johnson

One Sunday, as I was shaking hands with people as they left after service, a rather loud-spoken lady came to Ron who was mingling nearby, and suggested that I was much too old a wife for him and that he should divorce me and find someone younger. Poor Ron, taken quite aback by her forthrightness, sheepishly suggested to her that she have a good week and that he thought he would likely just hang on to the wife he already had.

Another blessing on our path was young man who told us he was Stonerock. We inquired, but nobody seemed to know what his real name was. Stonerock was often inebriated but he was a gentle soul who waffled between pensive angry moods where it was not unusual for him to stare contemplatively at one of his many treasured knives as he talked, and tender-hearted tears. He was not shy about letting his needs be known and we offered him bread and water on more than one occasion. He was always very appreciative. He didn't have any means of transportation so Ron gave him a bicycle. He was very proud of his bike and often came by to show us that he was taking care of it and riding it to the places he needed to go. We love Stonerock and hope to see him in heaven one day.

One evening we received a knock at the parsonage door. I answered. A man from the community whom we had seen at breakfast a time or two with a gentleman from the church stood before me with tears in his eyes. He shoved a piece of paper into my hand and exclaimed, "What do I do about this! Do something about this!" And he left. The piece of paper turned out to be a letter, unsigned, from a gentleman in my church. In essence the letter said that since the church member had treated him to breakfast on several occasions and had taken him to places of interest, that it was now time for more. Their relationship needed to move to a more intimate level. I didn't know for certain that the letter had been written by my church member until he read an announcement the next Sunday morning written on the same distinct writing paper. I prayed and agonized over what to do. I needed to respond. Ron, in his simple, wise way, gave me the answer. They were both grown men. Let them work it out themselves. I responded to the victim who had obviously been being groomed, letting him know that he needed to deal directly with the situation, set appropriate boundaries or else terminate the relationship. He received our counsel gratefully and respectfully, and as far as we know, ended the relationship. The Area Minister and I would be keeping a close watch on our beloved church member.

Second only to leading four people from our jail Bible study to Jesus, was the blessing of my ordination. Before I could be ordained however, I had to be examined by the Ordination

Council. Church officials along with other church members and our own church family gathered a month before my ordination. I was asked several questions by members of the Council, including questions about my relationship with my father, my deepest desire for ministry, and one very pointed eschatological question. Perhaps the most interesting question came from a general church member in attendance who asked how I would handle it when I applied for a church that rejected me because I am a woman. There was a stirring in the crowd when the question was asked and the Council Moderator said I didn't have to answer that question. I said I didn't mind at all and heard a hush fall over the crowd. My answer went something like this:

"Sir, thank you for your question. It's a very good one and one I will have to deal with at some point I am sure so I appreciate you asking it. What I hear, however, underneath that question, is another question. And to me it is a more important question, and that is, can anyone, specifically a church search committee, thwart God's will for my life. And the answer to that question, Sir, is an unequivocal, uncategorical, 'no.' When I believe this, then I can approach churches, and if they reject me, I know with absolute certainty that God has a better plan, and my only responsibility is to trust Him." There was a pregnant pause, a palpable sigh from the audience and a short, reserved applause.

With that, an Ordination Council member called for the adjournment of the Council and the Moderator closed in prayer.

Within a week, I received a letter telling me that the Ordination Council had recommended me for ordination and I could proceed with making plans for this sacred day. A week before my big day, I had the best gift ever. My sister called from Nova Scotia to ask if we could pick her up at the airport if she were to fly in for my ordination. I still get teary-eyed when I think of the distance she travelled to be with me on this very special day of my life. It was such a joy to have her with me. We prepared my ordination luncheon together, set the tables, and went shopping for my special outfit for the day. Oh, what joy to have your calling confirmed and affirmed by ordination. And, oh, what joy to share it all with the older sister you looked up to for your whole life. On a beautiful Sunday afternoon, November 12, 2006, I was ordained by my local church within the American Baptist Churches USA as a minister of God's Word.

The reality in the church I served, was that it was pressed beyond limit in maintaining the church and parsonage and providing adequate pastoral compensation. There were a few heated discussions at trustee meetings as to whether to pay the pastor or the light bill. There were times when my expenses or benefits like health insurance were delayed for months in favor of paying basic bills like heat and lights. I invested personal funds into advertising and marketing materials for the church and maintained a visible presence in the community and yet the church didn't grow. The visitors who did come, never stayed more than a few Sundays, leaving in favor of a fellowship with more children or youth, or a more active congregation. Part of the reality was simple logistics. This was a city of 3800 people and 22 churches. Strictly for analysis, I asked all of the pastors in town to tell me how many people they believed would claim the church they served as their church if they were asked. It was not a matter of attendance, but only how many claimed a specific church as the one they would attend if they did go, and from which they expected they would be married and/or buried. The total came to 4500! It was inevitable that I would need to look for another place of ministry.

Ron wanted desperately to be back in Minnesota. One conference I went to while we were in Nebraska was held at Sioux Falls, South Dakota close to the Minnesota border. On a break, I headed to the first rest stop just inside Minnesota. There, I stood on a grassy knoll and cried out to God. I asked first for his will to be done in our lives, but I also pleaded with him to take us back to Minnesota thinking maybe that would make Ron happy. He was trying very hard to be positive but the financial difficulties at the church had been weighing him down and he was feeling the stress of mounting credit card debt.

Gentle Love

It was hard to leave our little church in Nebraska. We knew the people loved us and we certainly loved them. Some were angry that we were leaving so soon, after only two years. Others were resigned and understood that supporting a full-time pastor was too hard for them.

12
TOUGH LOVE

The letter came sometime in the summer inviting us to dialogue about becoming their pastor. I didn't know the area so I asked Ron if it would be a good place to live and he was more than a little positive. The letter provided an email address so I emailed saying I was interested. Shortly after, we received an information package in the mail. The parsonage was a multi-level, four-bedroom home with a triple garage. The church was a congregation of a little less than 200 members comprised of American Baptist Churches (ABC) and United Church of Christ (UCC), in one of the most desirable areas in the state of Minnesota. Ron and I were filled with anticipation.

We took advantage of summer vacation to visit friends in Minnesota and meet with the search committee. We had a tour of the church and parsonage. We were overwhelmed by both. When we learned what the financial package was, we were again overwhelmed at our good fortune. We both felt that if I were accepted as the next pastor at this church, it would be a clear sign that God was rewarding us for our faithfulness during the previous two years. We also felt very much at home in the area when we visited and thought this would be a great place for a long and fruitful ministry. The salary would finally give us a chance to pay down those looming credit cards, and the farming area helped Ron to feel very much at home. Above and beyond those reasons, as soon as we walked into the church, I had a clear sense that this is where God wanted us to be. All indicators were in the direction of this being our next place of ministry. The sense of completeness, or rightness, of the place was so strong it was hard to explain. From the very first night when one of the search committee met us in the Menard's parking lot to show us to our hotel, we both believed this was God's perfect will.

A little later in the summer, we went again to the area. This time it was for me to candidate and for us to meet the congregation. Following the service, church members voted on whether to call me as their next pastor or not. The vote was overwhelmingly positive. Ron and I were thrilled. What we did not know was that the next two years would be the toughest we had ever faced.

Betty Anne Johnson

After our move, while I was still unpacking boxes and not officially started yet with the church, Ron had already begun working for a local farmer. We've always marveled at how God has provided for Ron's employment as Ron has sacrificed to allow me to follow my call to ministry. Even when his back went out, God provided another opportunity which was perfect for him. We were thrilled that now not only was he working, but he was doing what he had known all his life — farming. And we had arrived in September, just in time for harvest.

I was getting us nicely settled into our new home and me into my church office. The local newspaper called to do a story welcoming the new pastor to the area. I was excited about my first Sunday with my new church family. Within a few weeks I would have the privilege of welcoming nine new members into that church family. At the same time, however, I would receive an intriguing visit from an inured, seasoned church member.

He came to my office on a Tuesday morning. We'll call him Bill. He was older, well-spoken, had an air of confidence about him, and held an official position in the UCC, although he did not serve on any boards or committees of our church. He was pleasant enough. We chatted for a short while and then he said he had two things to talk to me about in order to help me understand what was required of me as pastor.

As was my custom, I encouraged the congregation to bring a Bible to church by asking for a show of Bibles and making a comment on how many or how few there may be. It has always been met with some enthusiasm and has always increased the use of personal Bibles during church services. The first thing Bill wanted to tell me was that we were an inclusive congregation and therefore I should not encourage people to bring their Bibles to church. This public affirmation of those who brought their personal Bible to church=made those who didn't bring a Bible feel less Christian.

The other matter had to do with altar calls. During one of the Sunday services of my three-week tenure, I had provided an opportunity for anyone who wanted prayer to come forward, I would pray for them, and they could then return to where they were sitting. One person came forward, stood with me, we had prayer, and she returned to her seat. Bill viewed this as an "altar call." He advised me that this type of action would make those who did not come forward for prayer feel "less Christian," so I should refrain from it. He also advised that since I was now serving as the pastor of a dual-affiliated congregation, I would need to apply for credentialed standing with the UCC.

When Bill left, I gave my head a shake and wondered what I had gotten myself into. If prayer and the Bible were that close to being taboo, what else did this congregation believe or not believe? I thought the search committee had asked relevant and meaningful questions during our time together. I knew Bill was a prominent, if not respected, member of the congregation. He had spoken to me of doing a Ph.D. I asked him the title of his dissertation and later looked up anything I could think of that would come close to what he had told me. I found nothing. He also told me during our visit that people tended to gossip about his being under cover with a federal agency. We chuckled over that.

I realized that Bill was only one member of the congregation, but I also knew that if one member had certain thoughts, it was quite possible other members might also have the same opinions, or at least be influenced in that direction. I looked up my requirements as an ABC pastor serving a dual-affiliated church. While it was recommended, it was not a mandatory requirement that I be credentialed with the UCC. I was relieved, since my theology did not align with that denomination's. I also discovered, during my research, that Bill's position with the UCC was as a member of the credentialing board.

Before I could give much more thought to my visit with Bill, I had another visitor. Rose (not her real name) was the daughter of a former pastor to the church. She had just moved back to the area and had met up again with the love of her life from high school days. Rose loved to sing and wanted to start a worship team for the church. I was thrilled at Rose's request but it is also in my nature to be cautious of anything so new. I told Rose she had my blessing to try to see how it would go. I told her we would evaluate it again in six months.

With a church of about 200 members, there was a lot to do every day. Several of our members were in the local nursing home or memory care facility. There was almost always someone in the hospital, and there were a few members who were otherwise healthy, but not mobile. A good portion of time, therefore, was spent in visiting people. There were also the administrative tasks of writing a monthly article for the church newsletter, getting information to the church secretary who worked most mornings, and attending various meetings of the church boards and committees. While it was a full schedule, it did not seem fraught with busyness. I keep good margins in my daily routine but it seemed there was always an undercurrent of discontent which erupted and required my time at least once every week.

The Praise Team was comprised of three or four people depending on the Sunday. There was one guitarist, and all of the team sang. Every other Sunday, they would stand before the congregation and sing two or three hymns or hymn choruses from the hymnbook. Hymnbooks were still in use since there was no visual equipment. I began to get regular visits or emails from the Praise Team about the fact that they practiced quickly on Sunday morning before service, and that Rose didn't seem prepared. I also had two church members who were not in the

Praise Team, mention to me that they thought Rose and her boyfriend were living together.

Within a few months of the Praise Team's debut, I asked to see Rose in my office. I had asked in passing during previous weeks, how things were going and she was always very positive about the cohesiveness and quality of the Praise Team. It was clear from simple observation that when the team sang, it was a 'dead spot' during the service and the congregation were not engaged with what was happening. I hoped they would improve with time, but knew I needed to address the concerns I had received.

When Rose and I met, I asked her directly if she was living with her boyfriend and she confirmed that she was. I asked her about her upbringing. Since her father was a Baptist pastor, I made the assumption, rightly or wrongly, that she would have been taught that living together while unmarried was wrong. Rose was moved emotionally by my question but insisted that she was not doing anything wrong. I suggested to Rose that until she was married, perhaps she would step down as the team leader. She told me that was not an option. I was about five months into my time with this congregation and felt that I had only one way to respond. I told Rose that we would need to put the Praise Team on hold for at least a while and we could talk more about it later. I prayed for Rose before she left but I could see she was not happy with me or my decision.

Rose's discontent manifested itself in a two-page, type-written letter to the board of deacons that same week. The letter included some pretty serious charges concerning my being judgmental and aloof. It suggested the church was moving toward being an unwelcoming and unloving church and one which was more than willing to "cast the first stone." The letter also indicated in closing that Rose had "sought the counsel of elders in the church" who she respected and trusted. I learned later, two of those elders were Bill and his wife.

With strong support from the Deacons' Board and positive reinforcement from many of the church members, I decided that the best course of action was to focus on ministry and pray for Rose and those who may be influenced by her discontent. Worship services returned to a regular schedule for the most part. We added members, participated in community services such as Thanksgiving and Good Friday, and enjoyed the fellowship of the two other churches in town through our joint vacation Bible school program.

There were, however, incidents that in hindsight were critical to what was brewing underneath. A more experienced pastor may have been alert to the incidents being a volcano about to erupt. I had my concerns, but naively thought that it was a few out of the many and things would settle as we got to know one another better. Maybe I had just forgotten that a little yeast works through the whole dough.

One Sunday morning as I rose to start the worship service, I noticed Rose at the back of the church by the sound booth. She had a microphone in her hand and was chatting to the sound operator. The chatter was quite animated, and seemed to center around whenever I was talking, not when we were singing. Rose had not been congenial since I put the Praise Team on hold and I had no idea what she was up to with a microphone in her hand at the back of the church. That same Sunday I was pleasantly surprised to see a new family in church - they took up a whole pew and sat fairly close to the front. I hadn't seen any of them around town but was looking forward to meeting them and seeing if they were new to the area. It seemed to me as if they were certainly checking us out since most of the family had their arms crossed and the one who appeared to be the father had a terrible scowl on his face. I thought perhaps he had been dragged to church!

When it came time for the offering, Rose came to the front and sang a solo for the offertory. I had no idea she had arranged to sing that Sunday. That was fine. She did a lovely job. When she finished, she sat with the "new family." After her solo, as I walked to the pulpit to preach, the scowl on the man's face deepened and I realized this family was related to Rose. The scowls from father and the rest of the family continued through the message and I learned later that this was Rose's immediate family. They had come to make a statement and make it they did! The man with the scowl had pastored the church many years before! After the service, the family made no attempt to meet me but headed directly to the fellowship hall where we always had refreshments. After the usual handshakes at the door, while I was gathering my things and putting my microphone away, I heard a man's voice coming from the fellowship hall as if he were addressing those in the room. I had my suspicions as to what was happening so I gathered my things and headed home. Ron told me later that it was the former pastor who had spoken to the people during fellowship. He had greeted "his people" but had also suggested to them that the content of my message that morning was in error.

Early in my tenure, before things got too tumultuous, we scheduled a new church directory to be completed within the year. The time came for the directory company personnel to arrive. They would be at the church for about three days to complete photographs and to give members an opportunity to purchase photo packages. Rose was one of the volunteers checking people in to their photo session appointment. Volunteering at the table next to her was a deacon of the church. Rose couldn't pass up the opportunity.

"Did you know Pastor Betty is working from home?" Rose asked. The deacon advised Rose that she did know I was working from home that week and that the deacons had agreed given the increased traffic flow at the church. Rose responded, "Well the secretary really needed her and she wasn't here."

The Sunday morning following this interchange, I started the worship service as usual. Rose generally sat toward the back of the sanctuary. This Sunday she sat more toward the front. As we began to sing, Rose's voice resonated well above mine and the congregation's. I have a strong voice but not as strong as Rose's. I softened my voice and allowed Rose to "lead" not wanting to engage in a power struggle right there and then. Following the service, my husband asked me what was "wrong" with Rose. Others also mentioned her intensity during the first hymn. To all, I simply responded, "She does have a strong voice."

It became increasingly clear that Rose was not going to rest until she had the Praise Team back up and running, or had removed me from my pastoral position. Deeper discontent was brewing. At a joint meeting of the Deacons' Board and the Pastoral Relations Committee, I was asked why I didn't say, "This *is* the body of Christ," and "this *is* the blood of Christ," during communion. I couldn't defend myself because I couldn't remember what exactly I had said at our previous communion time. I do sometimes say that the bread and wine are representative of the body and blood, but not always. Questions of infant baptism or dedication were also raised. I prefer infant dedication, but had already done two infant baptisms, so I was confused as to the call for affirmation that I was willing to do them.

The meeting was a long one and many of my actions, intentions, and motivations were questioned. There was good support and positive affirmation from several, along with no support and negative accusation from several. I was completely drained.

As a result of the tension, I started writing out everything I would say on Sunday morning and I stuck strictly to the script. I prayed that the Lord would release me from this position or help me see where there could be a breakthrough. I preached my heart out, had a foot-washing service, extended an invitation for people to come and talk with me and a deacon. The deacons continued to support me in my leadership. Other leadership and committees offered their support. The undercurrent of discontent seemed to be coming mostly from those who held no leadership positions within the church.

Soon Rose started spending time at the church whenever the secretary was there. The secretary started setting her own hours, often calling in to say she wouldn't be in as scheduled for various and sundry reasons. One morning she was to meet with the Personnel Committee. She came to work, but then just before the meeting, she left unexpectedly. When a member of the Personnel Committee called her, she advised him she had taken ill. There were several issues the Personnel Committee wanted to care for with the secretary but it seemed whenever they called a meeting, she was a no show, or she came with other church members who disrupted the meeting making it impossible to mutually resolve the issues on the table. Eventually the Personnel Committee decided they would have to terminate her employment. This resulted in a flurry of letter-writing among members with accusations against the church leadership and the pastor.

The first taxing year of what we thought would be a fruitful ministry experience escalated into a second stress-filled one as the flurry of letters continued despite responses from the Deacons' Board offering individual meetings or small group meetings. In January, I got a call from the ABC Executive Director letting me know that he had received a letter from 12 church members leveling charges of spiritual abuse against me. This type of letter automatically set into motion a process designated by the regional office. At the end of the month, there would be a meeting of the Nurturing Professional Leadership Ministry Team (NPLT) to determine the course of action to be taken.

Given the gravity of what was now facing me, I immediately called the chair of the deacons, who called the church moderator and the chair of the Pastoral Relations Committee. Within minutes, however, I received word from the regional office that all information regarding the matter should be kept confidential until the preliminary meeting of the Nurturing Professional

Leadership Team took place. The three people who had already been apprised of the situation were informed as to the confidential nature of the situation at this point. The whole "keep it quiet" until the denomination does what it needs to do triggered the feelings from years before of the spiritual abuse I had endured at the hands of another denomination. This time, however, it would be different. The response from the denomination provided a new reference point and another step in my journey toward wholeness.

On January 30, I received a phone call from the regional office advising me that the Nurturing Professional Leadership Team had unanimously agreed that the charges were not matters of misconduct and that a letter was on its way to the 12 members outlining their findings and recommendations. I was not to share this information with anyone until the letter had arrived from the NPLT.

My copy of the letter arrived on Feb. 5. I was absolved of any misconduct. The NPLT stipulated that the tension we were all experiencing was a matter of "compatibility of a ministerial leader and members of the congregation" and that these matters "are handled at the local church level." Prior to this incident, the church leadership and I had heartily welcomed the offer of the regional office to conduct a "Listening Conference" for the church community. The 12 signatories of the letter were encouraged to take part in that conference as part of the NPLT's recommendations.

Now I was advised by the regional office that I should inform the church leadership of what had just transpired so that they did not hear it from any of the 12, or sources other than me. I immediately called a special meeting of the Pastoral Relations Committee and the Deacon Board for the following two nights to ensure that everyone would be able to attend. The minutes of those meetings included the following:

Pastor Betty encouraged those at the meetings to continue to be positive about the future of our church and to give careful prayer about our response to those who signed their name to the letter. She emphasized the importance of a careful response rather than an emotional reaction to those involved.

A time for "processing" was offered at each meeting. After a time of prayer, care and concern, the meeting adjourned.

Note: the consensus of those at the meetings was that notes with attachments should be placed in the Deacon's binder as official record of these meetings and the letter from those 12 individuals.

When the January events and the resulting outcome became public knowledge, chaos erupted. I received dozens of emails and phone calls offering love and support. The deacons were inundated with questions. The 12 continued their protest, only now it was a public forum. Our small, tight-knit community was being forced to take sides in the debacle. The Board of Deacons wrote a letter to the 12 and they responded in kind. Some removed their membership from the church and in doing so, informed the church membership by way of letter outlining their reasons. Offers of personal meetings with the pastor and a deacon were either rejected or ignored. Everyone was encouraged to attend the listening conference the following month.

Considering the church size of 200, the Listening Conference had excellent participation. Seventy people participated and 60 individual listening sessions were held. The report by the denominational office concluded that the conflict within the church "goes back at least one decade and possibly as long as two decades." Reasons for the conflict included unresolved issues related to former pastors, theological diversity of the congregation, differing views on authority in the church, and an aging congregation. While the current conflict centered around the termination of the church secretary, all indications were that the tension was "more deeply rooted than this one event."

While the results of the conference allowed people to voice their hurts and fears to denominational leadership, it did not serve to alleviate them. Strong recommendations were offered in the Listening Conference report but to meet the desired outcome of the recommendations all those involved would need to communicate openly and honestly with the goal of reconciliation rather than "fighting to the death for their own personal vision of what the church should look like."

Following the conference, several people chose not to attend the church but did not remove their membership. Some left simply because of the conflict, not because they felt personally involved in it. Others, including at least three or four of the 12, chose to continue to attend faithfully. While the flurry of letter-writing slowed considerably, there was no tangible evidence of a move toward reconciliation. I received personal notes asking me to leave. I had one person ask me how much money it would take to get me to resign. I advised this well-meaning man that I could not be bought, and that I would leave when God released me to do so. The annual report of the deacons in referring to the recommendation of the Listening Conference, concluded, "We have not been successful in getting a concerted effort of our membership to put these suggestions to work and gain unity in (our church)."

Personally, the 18 months Ron and I had put in at the church had taken its toll. I gained considerable weight. Ron loved where he was working and appreciated the family for whom he was working. However, when he would come home and learn the kind of day I had, we would invariably head out for dinner and some comfort food. The work of the ministry— visiting, funerals, weddings, and worship services still had to be managed with care and compassion for everyone. I did the best I could while still writing out every word I would say on Sunday morning for fear of reprisal regarding something I might have said. At least I would have a record of what I actually did say. When I shook hands with people after service, a few would take the opportunity to correct my wording or offer a note of criticism about the message, something they perceived was not in line with the church's theology.

The regional ministerial of ABC pastors walked with me through every aspect of my journey. They expressed shock and concern and prayed for me faithfully. One pastor insisted that we needed to "pray them out." He meant well, and perhaps he was right. I would rather have seen reconciliation and movement toward godly unity than anything. I continued to be welcomed and cared for not only by my denominational brothers and sisters, but by the local ministerial as well. Two of the local ministers made special visits to my office to pray with me and offer me their love and support. One pastor, who was completing a 25-year tenure in anticipation of his retirement, advised me that "the first ten years are the hardest!" It was such a comfort to have his visit and tender-hearted presence. I emailed a previous pastor asking if we might have a phone conversation. I was hoping he could offer some help with the overall culture of the church or any insight into the personalities involved in the current conflict. His email response welcomed a phone conversation and he added that serving at the church had been the "most stressful time" of his life.

The months following the Listening Conference continued to be difficult with weekly or at least monthly criticisms and long letters of rebuttal to sermons or newsletter reports. Generally, things were more peaceful than before. A gentleman from the congregation offered to volunteer as secretary. During these months, however, I did begin the process of applying for other ministry positions. Ron and I really didn't want to leave the area. The sense of being at home had never left us despite the difficult situation. The churches I contacted were all in the Maritime Provinces of Canada. It was the only other place that I thought I would truly feel at home.

Besides my husband and my ministerial colleagues, the constant care of those in the church who were in key leadership roles along with other church members, provided the physical presence and nurturing to sustain me. Prayer was my best friend. The daily conversations with God about where, when and why consumed me. At the same time, my heart overflowed with gratitude that to the best of my knowledge there was nothing blocking my relationship with my Savior. There was no known unconfessed sin. My heart broke for Rose and Bill and others who were obviously hurt and scared that they were losing the church they knew and loved.

Early on in the fracas, I told one of the deacons that I could make it all better if I would just apologize to Rose and reinstate the Praise Team. But where would that leave the other two couples I had counseled to get married? Surely I would need to amend the teaching I had given them which they received so willingly. One couple asked me to baptize their baby but they were not married. After two beautiful visits with this lovely couple, they arranged for their baby's baptism and surprised their guests by getting married first. It was a joyful expression of God's love and a highlight of my ministry. No, compromising on the truth of God's word was never an option. However, I could have handled it differently. In giving Rose the go ahead to "try it," I opened the congregation to the potential joy of a Praise Team and the possible grief at its loss. I believe I would have been a better pastor to have protected the congregation from any significant changes like this one, with an unknown newcomer, until I had been at the church for at least a year, if not two.

The stress of trying to lead a deeply conflicted church taught me that my convictions ran deeper than my fears. My deepest longing as a pastor, apart from seeing those who don't know Jesus come to know Him, has been to see people grow in their faith and understanding of the beauty God has created in them as his image-bearers. The experience has also taught me, though, that fear often precipitates anger in people which can prevent them from working together to find the truth in any situation.

After the Listening Conference, I continued to serve for another ten months. The churches for which I applied called other pastors. No opportunities to move from my current ministry post were on the horizon. I was still in the process of transferring my ordination credentials but that entailed completing two courses by correspondence neither of which had yet been completed. Then one morning, sitting in my recliner during my quiet time with the Lord, he spoke.

It was a Wednesday. The house was quiet. Nothing particularly earth-shattering was on my agenda. I read my devotional reading and the accompanying scripture. I bowed my head to listen. It was my usual practice. It couldn't have been clearer if God had spoken audibly in the quiet of that moment: "It's time."

I knew exactly what he meant. It was time for me to resign. I sat in silence for several minutes as we communed together. Oh how sweet those moments were! I felt a peaceful sense of release envelop my soul and spirit, and I felt a contented joy that I hadn't felt in over two years, if ever.

I gently set my book and Bible on the side table and picked up the phone. I called the chair of the deacons and told him it was time. God had released me from my current ministry. Then I called the church moderator and told him I would be tendering my resignation the next Sunday morning, January 17, 2010. It coincided with the church's annual meeting.

Sunday morning came and I led worship as usual. Prior to the time for the message, I read my letter of resignation:

> *It has been a great joy for me to share in the spiritual growth of many sisters and brothers in the Lord in the past two years. God's graciousness in allowing me the strength to grow and mature in my leadership role has brought me tremendous blessing and joy.*
>
> *The past two years have been ones of continued conflict for (the church). Despite efforts to accommodate all members of the church through a Listening Conference, follow-up seminar, exhortation and encouragement, some members and non-members continue to level criticism at the current spiritual leadership.*
>
> *Today, therefore, I am announcing my resignation as Pastor of (the church).*

After I read my letter, I walked slowly but deliberately down the aisle and into my office across from the sanctuary. People began to move out of the sanctuary and down to the lower level fellowship hall for the annual meeting. As people came out, two obvious paths developed; those going directly downstairs and those coming to my office to wish me well, cry, offer a hug. To me, it seemed there was a steady stream of people to my office and I heard the Holy Spirit say, "This is your church." I didn't think much of it at the time as these precious people who were now offering me their love and support had been standing behind me for the past two years and four months. They were the church I had pastored for those two years.

People slowly cleared from the main level, and I joined the meeting downstairs which was already underway. As I walked in, I heard someone say, "But we don't have a pastor now." I spoke up right away and said that they had a pastor for the next 30 days. There was no response to my interjection and discussion centered around what could be done to carry on given the sudden departure of the pastor. At one point, a member called for recognition. He stood to say that he would like to tender his resignation as a member of the church and all boards or committees on which he was serving. As soon as he sat down, another member stood and reiterated the same sentiment. I decided this was a church matter, best left without interference from a departing pastor, so I left the meeting and went home.

By late afternoon, I learned that several key leadership positions, including the Moderator and chair of the Deacons' Board had resigned their positions and removed their membership from the church. A meeting was arranged for the following night to discuss the possibility of starting a new church in town. My heart shuddered but I wasn't surprised. A little over a year prior, I had received an email from a key leader in the church letting me know that he and his wife were thinking seriously of removing their membership and that they "intended to pursue the planting of a new church in (town)."

The following day, one of the deepest tragedies during my time in ministry confronted me. I received a call that one of our 16-year-old boys had been in a very serious vehicle accident and was being airlifted to hospital. This young man was a regular visitor to our home. He was Ron's "little buddy" and they doted on one another. I couldn't reach Ron at work so I waited until he got home and we headed to the hospital. The weather was making it difficult to get anywhere and a little over halfway to the hospital we learned that this young man had died. We turned around and headed to his parents' home to await their arrival. They would be returning from the hospital after being out of town for the weekend.

I did not attend the meeting about a church plant, but 25 others did and they decided to start a new church in town, affirmed their commitment, and set the wheels in motion for the following Sunday. I was asked to pastor the new church but was hesitant to do it. Perhaps I should have said a categorical, "no" right from the beginning, but something stirred within me. My former church had already told me they did not expect or want me to fulfill my 30 days notice. The Spirit's voice, "This is your church," the previous Sunday took on new meaning for me and I wondered what exactly God was up to and if, as unorthodox as it might be, he might be telling me to stay. These precious people had been like sheep without a shepherd for so many years. I told the group that I would at least be there for them as long as we were in town and that I would be willing to help them with their initial start up. The organizers for the new church did most of the administrative tasks of letting people know what was happening. I arranged for the rental of the local community hall. It only took a week. By Sunday, Jan. 24, they were ready for their first service.

It wasn't enough that I had resigned and left my former church. Those who had taken up the leadership positions left open by the exodus the previous Sunday, were determined to not just have me gone, but to get me decommissioned from ministry. Bill, the one who had written the most letters and who had led the 12 through their various processes, advised the Executive Minister of the ABC that those who had left the church had done so under my leadership, that it had all been pre-planned, and that the community hall where we were to hold services had been booked prior to Sunday's meeting. The Executive Minister called me to confirm the story. I told him it was not true.

Despite my assurance that these new accusations were false, he said in order to maintain my standing with the ABC, I would need to meet with a ministerial committee for review. After the previous two years, it all felt like too much. Ron was home when I received the call. When I got off the phone, I simply melted. I had reached the point of no return. I couldn't face another meeting, another accusation, another tribunal. Ron asked me what my options were and I told him I had to meet with them or relinquish my standing. Ron's reply was:

"Then do it."

"What?"

"Do it. Let your standing with them go. Then you won't need to deal with them."

So I did. In February at a Pastors' Retreat for the denomination to which I was hoping to transfer, I spilled the whole long story to the District Superintendent. He listened with empathy, but I thought he might discontinue the process, and I would have to start looking for a denominational home all over again. But he saw the thing I had suspected for two years. And someone else saw it too: the Catholic priest in our town.

At a ministerial meeting where we were welcoming a new pastor to the area, the question arose as to the number of churches in the parish we served. The new pastor served a two-point parish. The Catholic priest served a three-point parish. I said I was serving just one church. The priest said that I had just left a two-point parish. I looked at him quizzically and he continued, "You served two churches in the same building!" He couldn't have been more accurate and his words encouraged my heart and soul beyond what he will likely ever know this side of heaven.

Looking back at the most difficult two years of my ministry experience, I realize the essence of the contradiction. In serving one church family well, I automatically served the other family poorly. I was ill-equipped, and incapable of serving a UCC church. Not all UCC churches are on the denominational roster as "open and affirming" but the denomination encourages and supports the LGBT+ lifestyles and practices. Church culture, theology and personality vary from state to state. I'm also quite sure that many, if not most, UCC churches would encourage attendees to bring their Bibles to church and many may even encourage public times of prayer. The ABC church I served in Nebraska could have been called conservative evangelical. There are ABC churches in Minnesota that are supportive of practicing LGBT+ friends.

During my 28 months at the ABC/UCC church, the camp director of one of the UCC camps transitioned from male to female and continued to serve as camp director. All UCC churches were sent a letter from the denomination requesting support and encouragement for the transition.

Since God has given us the mandate to love one another, and since I believe the practice of homosexuality is inconsistent with Biblical principles, and because it is important for Christians to bring their Bibles with them when attending church, and since prayer is an important and vital part of corporate worship, I admit that during my time at this particular church, I blew the lid off the pressure cooker and caused a ruckus from which only God would be able to bring beauty and joyous love. Those two churches of which my Catholic friend spoke, now reside, minister, and cooperate in the same community. They just weren't meant to live together.

13
JOYOUS LOVE

Ron and I were still unsure of whether we should stay in town or not. If we stayed, we would need to buy a house in a hurry. We had 90 days to vacate the parsonage so April was our deadline. We explored possibilities in other areas, talked about moving back up north, or to Canada. Ron talked about getting a truck and going into business for himself. He was still working for the farming family that he started with the first week we arrived from Nebraska. While all of the options before us were viable, none of them specifically enticed us, or stirred our spirits as the next path God was laying before us. We kept our eyes open for houses on the market in town. When the Lord provided just the right place for us, and the purchase was finalized in late

March, the decision was made and our church family breathed a collective sigh of relief.

The church was flourishing. It was a happy place with so much energy. After the first Sunday service, we named the church. Everyone got involved in the fun and lively discussion and there was unanimous agreement. We would be called Faith Bible Church. Faith, because we were stepping out in faith. Bible, because we were committed to the truth of God's Word. Church was chosen over a more generic "chapel" or "center" because there was a resounding declaration that we were to always be a church because Jesus said he would build his church, not a chapel, or a country club!

One man made a communion table which doubled as a storage cupboard. The community hall gave us permission to leave it at the building. Another man made a mobile sound booth which he faithfully brought each Sunday until the community hall graciously found space for us to store it also. Donations poured in for the necessary church accessories. Worship was spirited and lively. Children sat at round tables toward the back of the community hall. Older adults sat in rows of chairs at the front of the hall. Children and adults worshiped together. Sunday School was a one-room schoolhouse with classes scattered at tables. The little ones sat cross-legged on the floor with their teacher. Everyone worked together to make sure everything worked. We set up chairs and equipment every Sunday morning and at the end of the service, everyone helped by folding their own chair and putting it back where it belonged.

The community hall was equipped with a kitchen, so there was no problem having pot blessings (our term for pot lucks). Our rent for the community hall was also a nice boost for the city. The regular income allowed them to make some improvements which included a big outside sign with the names of the organizations who met there and at what time. We started with about 30-40 people our first Sunday and quickly grew to an average regular attendance of 60. The growth was great but our rental arrangements made it difficult to have any extra events or regular programs. Within a year, we started talking about how nice it would be to have a place of our own.

Every now and again a potential dedicated place of worship would present itself but there was nothing tangible until, in God's timing and provision, the perfect place became available. It was a little over two years since we had been established as Faith Bible Church and the pharmacist in town decided to retire and sell the pharmacy building. The building was one story with no basement, had two small rooms which could easily be used as classrooms, a larger room which could be used for larger meetings, a beautiful big open area for the sanctuary and a small kitchen, plus two bathrooms. Before there was any official notice about the pharmacy being for sale, we approached the pharmacist expressing our interest.

Once it was announced, there was a great deal of interest in the property. One Christian business owner who was very interested in more space withdrew his bid when he realized we were hoping to get it. He was not a member of our church but as a Christian brother, he recognized our need and God's work in progress. This is "the stuff" of the true catholic church. Another local large business in town wanted to acquire the building and made an offer above the asking price. God was in control and as two board members and I talked with the pharmacist one day outside the building, he told us he had chosen to sell his building to us. To God be the glory!

We were more than excited to realize that we might have a building to call our own. The only thing that might stand in the way was finding the funds for a down payment. So we took a vote. The vote was not about whether we wanted the building — everyone agreed that we did. The vote was with our pocketbooks. We needed a $20,000 down payment. When the need was presented, we got promises for $44,550. We needed operating costs of $10,800 over and above our budget and we got over $14,000. It was a financial miracle for our little congregation. To say the church family was excited when the results were announced would be an understatement indeed!

Betty Anne Johnson

With the building purchased in late Spring, the retrofit began and excitement mounted not just among the church members but within the community as well. When the retail shelves were removed from the building, we all marveled at the excellent condition of the carpet. When the kitchen crew went to buy a few items for the kitchen and they found a whole set of cupboards for less than half their original cost, we rejoiced. When a donation of chairs came from a church to the north, and tables, a cross, and altars came from a church to the south, we were in awe. When the sound system sprang to life and only one of the hand-welded connectors was dead, we celebrated. When painting was done, and piano, pulpit, and projector were all in place, we knew it was time to worship, and worship we did! Our first service in our newly renovated building was filled with the joy of the Lord. This was the Lord's doing and we knew it full well. The community could see we were a "real" church and we weren't going anywhere anytime soon.

Having a dedicated worship facility meant we could participate more fully in community events. We soon found a niche during the town's main winter event as we served hot apple cider and Christmas cookies to everyone who came by to warm up from the cold. Soon it was expected that FBC would be the Snowflake Dazzle "warming house." During Town and Country Days in the summer, the workers with the carnival brought their campers and used our water and electricity, which we were happy to share. Our front parking lot was used for a car show. On occasion a family or organization would ask to use our beautiful but very practical facility for a special event. Each of these gestures was a way of showing pride in our community and a spirit of sharing the good things God had so graciously provided for us.

One of the highlights of ministry is seeing young people grow to adulthood and be grounded in the faith. We had in our church family a young lady who was an older teen and part of our youth group. She was a sweet, capable young woman who completed high school and went to college to study culinary arts. She stayed at home during college but that didn't keep her from meeting Mr. Right while she was studying. This young couple were faithful to the church and we celebrated their engagement. As part of their preparation for married life, and because a good opportunity presented itself, they bought a home together several months before their wedding. One Sunday morning, the bride's concerned mom talked to me about their plans to move in together before their wedding. Buying a house would certainly present a strong temptation to live together regardless of the wedding date. I assured her mom that I would talk to her.

Betty Anne Johnson

I sent an email to this precious young lady whom I had come to know and deeply love. I reminded her of her commitment to God and of her commitment as a church member. I asked her if we might get together for a talk. It seemed like a long time before Clara got back to me but she accepted my invitation and suggested a place where we could meet. Both Clara, and her fiancee, Nate, were there when I arrived. I was a little nervous about how they might react to me calling them to their responsibility under God and the church. I had been hoping and praying that they would both have teachable hearts.

We ordered our food and made small talk for most of the meal. Then Clara reached in her oversized bag and pulled out a book type calendar. There was no leading up to it. There were no questions. She simply got out her calendar, pointed to a date, and said, "We were thinking about October 12th." I was so blessed, I could hardly keep my composure. I had promised this young couple that I would do whatever I could to support them so that they could be married before they lived together. They had obviously talked about it and decided to follow the principles they had both been taught from a very young age.

God often blesses us beyond anything we could ask or think. The date Clara and Nate had picked was my own anniversary date! And it was a Sunday. One of the most beautiful things I could imagine was to be married as part of a worship service. Since I was doing a series of messages on what we believed and why, I asked Clara and Nate what they would think about getting married at the end of our service on marriage. They thought it was a great idea and they decided to surprise everyone except their parents and grandparents who "just happened" to be in church that day.

As I came to the close of my message on the beauty of a godly marriage, just three weeks after Clara and Nate and I had met, I announced that we were going to have a wedding right there and then and invited the bride and groom to come forward. You could hear the surprised murmurs ripple across the congregation. One person in the front row said right out loud, "Now?" I responded, "Yes, right now!" Everyone was smiling. The joy of that day was so beautiful as these two young people pledged their love and commitment to one another and to God. God is good beyond what we can ever ask or think!

One of the greatest joys for a pastor is to see those who have accepted Christ as Savior take the confirming step of faith to be baptized. Since our church was a former retail store, it wasn't built with a baptistry in mind, much to my delight. I've always felt that baptisms need to be outside in public, if at all possible. After we moved into our new facility, we got creative with having a public baptism, and having it in town. We set up a swimming pool in the church parking lot, and on one very special Sunday morning, following worship, we all headed to the parking lot where young and old alike, made public profession of their faith in Jesus Christ and were immersed in the waters of baptism. The swimming pool was drained, and put away, but the joy of that baptism never fades.

We held two more baptisms in a nearby lake. The first was a beautiful expression of God's faithfulness in the baptisms of a father and daughter. The other was the most meaningful baptism of my ministry experience. It was held on the afternoon of my last Sunday at FBC. I can think of no better way of finishing a season of ministry to a loved and cherished church family than with a baptism. The joy that day was palpable as each baptism candidate was gently and purposefully led into the water. For each of them, eternity had changed. For me, life would never be the same.

14
HOME

After 20 years in the USA, Ron reluctantly agreed that he would finally get me back to my beloved Nova Scotia. He was hesitant because we both had good jobs and were leaving them for completely unknown prospects. Also, the poor man had never had much luck when he ventured to the east coast. The first time we visited there, he thought he had lost me to a motorcycle accident. The second time we came, we had to replace all four tires on our camper and he broke his ankle. He just didn't have a really good feeling about moving to the east. Nevertheless, he said I had put in my time in the USA, so now he was willing to put in his time in Canada.

It wasn't easy to say goodbye to our Midwest friends. We had spent almost ten years in one place. Ron had done ten harvest seasons with his farming family who were more friends than employer. But the call toward home was strong as I inched closer to my mid-60's. I felt God had released me from ministry, and I was experiencing the effects of burn-out, not because of any conflict but simply the rigors of pastoral life.

I had been an integral part of the search process for a new pastor. I had given the church family almost a year's notice, so we were able to work together each step of the way. The Sunday after they released me with their warm and gracious blessing, they celebrated their new shepherd's arrival. I left knowing my sheep were not without a shepherd.

As I slipped behind the wheel of my Dodge Journey, with Ron in his truck with a cargo trailer hitched behind, I was almost giddy with anticipation of what lay ahead. The dream which I had held since my childhood was finally becoming a reality. I imagined us settling into a nice home on a quiet street somewhere in town. I would renew old acquaintances and Ron would make some great Christian friends with whom he could ride motorcycle. I would finish my doctoral project in the year ahead. We had agreed and budgeted for me to have a year off for just that purpose. I expected Ron would find a good job as soon as he got his work permit. I would write and take care of our home, and our evenings and weekends would be filled with together time with each other and with family who would stop by.

Home

The miles clicked by. The Midwest faded. The east coast came into view.

We spent the first two months of our new life on the east coast living with my sister and brother-in-law. That two months was filled with house hunting, transferring driver's licenses, and starting paperwork for Ron's permanent residence status. There was also a trip to the Midwest to load our household goods from storage into a U-Haul truck, drive back to the east and unload them into local storage.

Finding a house proved more difficult than we anticipated. We wanted a small house but with a big garage for Ron! We made an offer on one house but neither buyer nor seller would budge, so we settled for a mobile home to be set up on a double lot we purchased in a village just outside my hometown. Ron had his dream garage built on the property.

There was only one problem with where we lived, the noise. Ron knew I needed to live somewhere quiet. He had driven to the property before we bought it and sat in his truck with the door open for about 20 minutes and he said it was so peaceful. Unfortunately he did that one mid-afternoon for the rare 20 minutes when the road we fronted onto was quiet.

Betty Anne Johnson

For two years, dump trucks, semis, and speeding vehicles whizzed past our home at all hours of the morning and night. It was not unusual to hear loud pipes at 2 or 4 a.m. In addition to the road noise, an airport was located to the west of us and a train track to the east. We literally had the constant companionship of planes, trains, and automobiles. The barrage of traffic noise was so unrelenting, it became torturous for me. Life in my beloved Nova Scotia was nothing like I had hoped. Sitting outside was impossible. Conversations outside were impossible. It was quieter in the garage than the house. I just wanted it to stop!

Ron reluctantly agreed that we could sell in the coming Spring of our first year. We listed with a realtor but nothing happened. I would have to endure another year. The next Spring we listed with another realtor and this time we were able to sell the property. The house we had made an offer on two years before, was still for sale but at a lower price, so we made another offer and this time the house became our home.

Our new home is a beautifully peaceful and quiet property with a treed back yard, a sprawling front yard and a small but adequate garage. We have what one friend calls a Hallmark address. Ice Pond Drive does seem like a rather romantic place to live. We have friendly neighbors and plenty of wildlife to keep us company. The blue jays and cardinals gently wake us in the morning, and deer are regular visitors to our yard. In this idyllic setting it is almost possible to look back over the past three years and smile. Almost. Not quite.

While our plans were for me to have a year off in order to work on my doctoral project, within our first few months, I accepted the call to pastor the small village church where we had bought our first home. With the level of noise where we were, it was likely best that I had both pastoral work and my doctoral project to occupy my mind.

On the morning of December 23rd, three days before my sister's side of the family would gather at our place for Christmas dinner, I was working in my home office when the UPS driver arrived with the last book I needed for my doctoral research. Since our little Shih Tzu, Max, was uncomfortable with visitors, I most often noticed when a visitor arrived and met them at the door. That morning, I must have been concentrating hard and didn't expect the driver to arrive at 8:20. The doorbell rang. I came from one end of the house, and Max came from the other end, barking his usual high-pitched warning of invasion. I opened the door to greet the UPS driver and to let Max out for his morning business. Within a minute, Max came back across the threshold but his back legs were going out from under him. I assumed his little legs were cold from going from the warm bed to the winter outside, so I picked him up and took him to my husband to look after while I finished with the UPS delivery. I needed to pay some import fees so after I did that and we chatted for l moment, we wished one another Merry Christmas and I yelled to Ron that it was "okay" — the UPS driver had gone. That usually meant that Max would come bounding to the door again and bark or growl at the closed door like he had missed protecting us. Silence.

I thought Ron might not have heard me, so I said again that it was okay and headed to the room where I found Ron holding our "baby" in his arms. The saddest face I've ever seen on my husband met me. "I think he's gone," he said.

"No!" In one step I was beside Ron. I lifted Max's head and saw those beautiful big brown eyes looking straight at me. It seemed as if they were looking right through me.

"Oh, Max!" I took him and cradled him in my arms, then laid him on his blanket on the bed. I knelt beside him and stroked his lifeless body. Ron stood quietly at my side. After some time, we called the vet and made arrangements for Max. When we took him to the vet, we put Max in the back of my Journey wrapped in his blanket. I have no idea why I didn't cradle him in my arms on the way to the vet, and to this day I regret that I didn't. I often tear up when we drive past the animal hospital where we took him the day he died. It triggers the regret, and reminds me of my empty arms during that drive, and Max alone in the back, a spot too far away from us for him to ever be content.

"He's gone, Dear." The message from my sister-in-law burned my eyes as I looked at the text as I was wrapping up teaching my Music Appreciation class Thursday afternoon. I stifled my emotion, gave the girls their homework, dismissed class, and headed for my office. It was April 26, 2018.

The year before, I had resigned my pastoral charge to accept the position as principal/teacher at a local Christian private school. Not only was I thrilled to learn I had been accepted for the job, it was a dream come true. For many years I had wanted to work in education. I had had part-time opportunities and loved every minute. Now, for the past school year, I had been Principal to 80 students and team leader to a group of amazing teaching staff and volunteers. The year had been fraught with difficulties but I absolutely loved my job. And now the school year was coming to a close and we were already gearing up for the next year. It was also the year that in late November we received a phone call that my brother had stage 4 cancer.

My brother and I had always been close. We gave each other permission to be who and what we were. Since he was younger, I never imagined life without him. He had changed over the years, as had I. But we never lost the bond we developed sometime during our adulthood. No matter what he did, or what I did, we could always be real with one another. When I learned he was dying, I was angry. I was angry because we had been in Nova Scotia for almost two years and never had a visit. But then we had always just let the other live their life. I had expectations of how it would be when we moved closer to family, but it didn't happen, and I was angry. But the futility of fury melted into making the best of the time we had, so I began to visit often. As we knew the time was getting short, I visited every day after work. I knew the text would come. I had said my long goodbye the day before. He had slept most of my visit but I talked to him and we shared some special moments. I left my visit that day with a sense that it was my last. Ron called shortly after I left and I told him he needed to come if he wanted to see Jim one more time. I turned the car around and came back to the house with Ron. When Ron came in, Jim opened his eyes wide and said, "Oh! Ronnie's here!" Jim loved my husband and they became good friends during Jim's final months. I still miss him terribly, and I'm still just a little angry about what to me feels like time lost that we could have had.

One month later to the day, I was told that my contract at the school would not be renewed. No discussion. My broken heart broke again.

Home

    In the middle of our grief and brokenness there is always something for which we can be thankful. I'm thankful for my brother. I'm thankful for those final weeks where visits were so sweet. I'm thankful for the year that I had to exercise my passion for teaching and preparing lessons and looking into the sweet, innocent eyes of a struggling student to encourage him, or the lost look of a young lady who felt left out as she formed and developed her own opinions of who she is and what she wants to be. I'm thankful for my husband who goes to work faithfully each and every day, while I set the schedule and pace for my day according to my whims and moods. And I'm thankful that in all these things, God works to bring good out of all of our messes.

15
LOOKING BACK

Now that I'm in my retirement years, I struggle, along with everyone else at this stage of life I expect, with questions of meaning in life, and even with belief. It's easy when you're 30 or 40 years old, to sing about heaven and trusting God, and eternal life. But when earthly life gets defined by the next ten years, the reality of your own personal mortality takes on a whole new perspective. When you have more memories than goals, your hope for the future changes from earth-bound to eternity-bound.

If I really believe life after death is better than anything I could imagine, then why do I hold on to this life so tightly? If the shortness of this life pales in comparison to eternity, why do I want just one more day? Do I really believe, or have I been a fake my whole life?

Looking Back

Looking back, there are days when I would give just about anything to be back in the choir room at Bethany Bible College hearing Mr. Mealy give me one last word of advice. He told me he only had one thing to say to me — that I was gullible. Even though now I know the meaning of the word, I still don't really know what Mr. Mealy meant when he told me that. And hearing him say that I'm gullible is not what makes me long to go back. It's that back then I was innocent and, well, gullible. There was so much I had to learn, and yet I thought I knew so much. There was so much life ahead and yet I thought I had lived quite a bit. The days I feel that I'd like to go back, is so that this time I could get it right.

But there's a strange and perverse lie that captures the imagination of many Christians in going back and doing it right. It's a guilt trip that comes alarmingly close to a wolf in sheep's clothing. Going back and getting it right suggests that there were places in our lives where God wasn't with us, where God didn't guide our steps and keep our feet from falling. But the truth is, God is, and always was, with us. He guides our feet and he protects us from ourselves.

God knew every detail of my life before I was formed in my mother's womb. He knew the bad choices I would make. He knew the trouble I would get into. He knew how gullible I would be. But God also knew that every step I took he could use to create a masterpiece of beauty. Maybe this is one of those places where God's love is the richest. When we look back and realize in all that we've done and in all that we've tried to do, despite our very best, and worst, efforts, God was there, not forcing us into choices and actions, but fashioning our choices and actions, right or wrong, into something beautiful that would bring him the greater glory, if only our heart was in the right place. Maybe that was what Jesus was trying to tell us when he said that we can only see what people look like from the outside but God sees what is in a person's heart.

I could have made better choices, but God knew I wouldn't. So he took the life he knew I would lead, and he fashioned it into something that would bring him honor and glory because that was the longing of my heart. When I was too sure of myself and told God, "I've got this!" it was because I wanted to show him the glory he would get if I just ran full-speed ahead. Gullible. When I tried to live according to the biblical principles I had been taught, and I got caught in the trap of denominational bureaucracy. Gullible. When my passion teetered precariously close to pride, and I set people's teeth on edge. Gullible. When pride kept the secrets my heart wanted rid of. Gullible. Then Gullible looked back and saw God in every moment, every step, every bad choice, every hurt, every success, every failure, and there, Gullible met Grace and God's glory broke through.

16
AUTONOMY

Don't worry, I'll handle it was the cry of my soul
"Little Miss Efficiency" was my name and my goal
For every situation, life storm or trial
I was the one who would go the extra mile
You could count on me to get the job done
With a smile on my face another victory one
If you want something done, do it yourself,
That was my motto, no dust on my shelf!
I'd gladly do it to get it done right,
And I did it all, with all of my might.
And all that I was, was all that I did,
But deep down inside, my self was hid.
I was bruised and scarred and battered and sore,
But performance kept asking for more and more.
It took no account that my vessel was weak
Its relentless demands just caused me to seek
Some answer, some method, some way to survive
The death of my spirit, yet still look alive.
'Til finally it crumbled, the clay on the floor,
The vessel was broken and useful no more.

Betty Anne Johnson

There was no cry of anguish as I lay in the dust,
Just a parched, feeble whisper, "Lord, help me to trust."
And there on the floor of the dark potter's shed,
A soft, gentle voice said, "Don't move, rest your head."
And somehow I knew as he stroked my hair
That I could abide in His loving care.
So I laid there in silence, and before very long
I heard him say, "In your weakness, I'm strong."
He spoke of my worth as a daughter of God,
As he picked up the pieces of my broken facade.
And with all of my ugliness, hatred and shame
He carried me gently to the Potter's wheel again.
And now as he shapes and molds me each day,
A more radiant beauty comes out through the clay.
And I can rejoice as I sing a new song,
I'm a child of the King. To the King I belong.

© Betty Anne Johnson

You can find more poems by Betty in her book of poetry, titled, *If I Had Known:Family Poetry* available at Amazon.

ABOUT THE AUTHOR

Rev. Dr. Betty Johnson has a Bachelor of Sociology, a Master in Counseling, and a Doctor of Ministry. She is a retired, ordained minister. Betty lives with her husband, Ron, in Truro, Nova Scotia, Canada.

http://womanpastor.ca
http://www.amazon.com/author/bettyannej

Made in the USA
Columbia, SC
29 November 2019